METALS IN BOATS

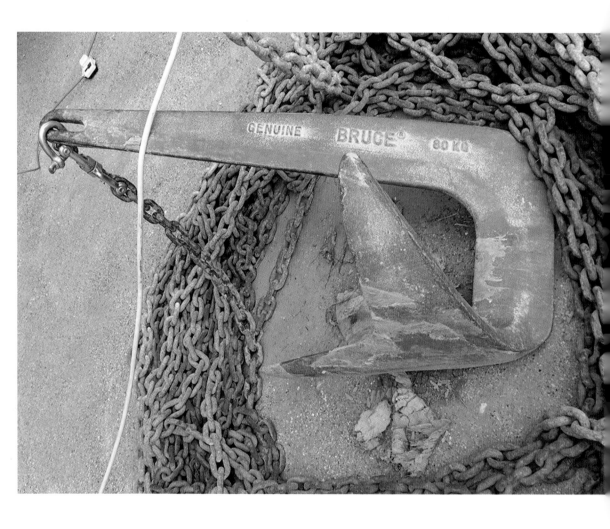

METALS IN BOATS

VYV COX

THE CROWOOD PRESS

First published in 2017 by
The Crowood Press Ltd
Ramsbury, Marlborough
Wiltshire SN8 2HR

www.crowood.com

British Library Cataloguing-in-Publication Data
A catalogue record for this book is available from the British Library.

ISBN 978 1 78500 262 5

Typeset by Manila Typesetting Company

Printed and bound in India by Replika Press Pvt Ltd

Contents

Foreword

For more than a decade Vyv Cox has been *Yachting Monthly*'s go-to man when it comes to technical features with an engineering slant. More often than not these features showcase Vyv's expertise in metallurgy, explaining to *YM*'s readers how the properties of different metals can change in the harsh marine environment, and what that might mean for them and their boats.

Vyv first approached us after narrowly escaping disaster when his anchor connector failed – he reasoned that if it could happen to him, it could happen to other cruisers. On our behalf he conducted rigorous destructive tests on anchor connectors and shackles. The results identified the best – and the worst – on the market, and he interpreted his results to demonstrate to *YM*'s readers what it was that made one better than another. Vyv's appetite for destruction was also brought to bear on C-links, used to join lengths of anchor chain, on anchor chain itself, and on Dyneema soft shackles.

When conducting our 'Seacock Safety' campaign, we drew heavily on Vyv's knowledge of dezincification to understand why some simple brass seacocks, skin fittings and hose tails failed so soon in their life cycle, often with dramatic results. Thanks to Vyv, this was one of our more successful campaigns. Having been convinced by his articles that brass seacocks just weren't up to the job, several boatbuilders changed from brass to stronger, safer DZR fittings, and manufacturers who then made only brass fittings were persuaded to switch to DZR.

Again it was to Vyv we turned when reports arrived in the office of bent shanks on a popular brand of anchor, raising fears that corners were being cut with the grade of steel used. For a specific production period, it transpired that these fears were well founded, but the dust never quite settled until Vyv conducted a full destructive metallurgical analysis on a new anchor and proved that current models now met the original design specification.

From keelbolts, spars and rigging, to ground tackle, rudder stocks and engines: metals play a major part in sail cruising. For most of us, metal is metal. It is strong and, provided that we replace our anodes in good time, we don't need to worry about it. The truth is that very bad things can happen, and have happened, when metals, salt water, fatigue and stray current come together. This book, with its concise explanations, clear illustrations and hard data, will help you understand the potential pitfalls. Adjust your maintenance regime – even the way you use your boat – and you'll steer clear of every one. This book will save you money. It could save your life.

Chris Beeson, Sailing Editor,
Yachting Monthly

Introduction

For nearly thirty years I worked for a multinational oil company, based initially near Chester, then later in Aberdeen and The Hague. During this period I carried out failure diagnosis on a wide variety of engineering equipment used in the production of oil and its refined products, including engines, pumps, compressors and gas turbines as well as static equipment. As all engineers will have experienced, during the course of this work I acquired detailed knowledge of associated peripheral subjects, particularly lubricants, elastomeric seals, bolts and bearings. Towards the end of my career I travelled extensively worldwide, troubleshooting and investigating problems in this vital equipment.

Upon retirement I transferred my expertise to the world of yachting, carrying out failure diagnosis for owners and in some cases writing about them for yachting magazines, principally *Yachting Monthly*. As time went by I also carried out destructive testing on behalf of this magazine, looking in particular at anchors and anchoring equipment.

Throughout my time at work and later I have been an active participant in yachting forums, where I found a ready source of failed components for (unpaid) consultancy supplied by many owners who had experienced failures on their yachts or who had been given suspect information by boatyards, boat builders and other owners. I created a website in which to share this information with all yacht owners at http://coxengineering/sharepoint.com.

Throughout my period at work and since I have been called upon to share my knowledge in talks, presentations and lectures. Since retirement I continued for some time with training in my professional topics but more recently this activity has also turned to yachting. Several times per year I am asked by yacht clubs, RYA local areas and Cruising Association sections to speak on a variety of subjects, but anchoring and failed components in particular. During a couple of these occasions I have shared the stage with the well-known broadcaster and yachtsman Paul Heiney, who suggested that I might like to write a book entitled *Metals in Boats.* I took up his suggestion, and here it is.

My thanks therefore go to Paul Heiney, Dave Lovejoy and Phil Gallagher for proofreading; my wife, Jill, for constant support and for more than her fair share of proofreading; but most of all to the members of ybw.com yachting forums and readers of my website who very kindly provide me with a vast range of interesting metallic problems and photographs to accompany them. I hope I have acknowledged you all but if I have omitted any please accept my apologies.

CHAPTER 1

Metal Facts and Properties

Modern boats depend heavily upon a wide range of metals for specialist fittings such as masts and spars, cleats and fairleads, nuts and bolts, in addition to the more mundane items such as engines, chain and anchors. Even in these parts the range of metals can be astonishing, with more specialism appearing annually. Selection of the correct metal for each task is rendered difficult because it not only has to give optimum performance in the application but also offer resistance to that ever-present corrosive medium, seawater. Even when it has been selected to satisfy these criteria it may perform poorly when attached to another metal due to the possibility of galvanic corrosion. Given the wide range not only of alloy compositions but also their manufacturing method, heat treatment and control of grain size, a good understanding is needed before specifying any metallic part.

In attempting to steer the user through the most common metals and alloys in service, this book will cover many terms with which the non-metallurgist is unfamiliar. Many specialist terms have entered general usage incorrectly, perhaps the word 'alloy' being one of the worst examples. To the vast majority 'alloy' means aluminium wheels on a car, or is used even by people who should know better, for example yachting journalists, just as a synonym for aluminium. The truth is very different. So

without going into detailed metallurgy I will start with an explanation of some of the terms that will be used throughout the book.

ALLOY

When two molten metals are mixed together and allowed to solidify, one of two things may happen. They will either be immiscible and solidify separately, or they will form an alloy. Sometimes the alloy will be a simple solid solution, in which a single phase of the same composition is formed, or in others a far more complex alloy is produced comprising several phases. Phases in metal alloys have differing compositions formed from the elements in the alloy. They are typically named according to the Greek alphabet, α, β, γ and so on, but of course the α phase in one alloy has a different composition from an α phase in another. Phases are commonly altered by heat treatment, affecting the properties of the alloy.

Variations in the proportions of the two component metals will affect the phase structure of the final alloy, for example when 70 parts of copper and 30 parts of zinc are mixed to form a 70/30 brass the result is a single α phase, whereas a 60/40 brass has a duplex $\alpha + \beta$ two phase structure and a 40/60 brass also has a duplex structure but of β + γ composition. The properties of the alloy depend upon the phases present, in the case of brass the α phase being more ductile but the β phase being stronger.

There are other possibilities, such as the formation of intermetallics, which will be touched upon briefly when galvanizing is discussed. In all cases a commercial alloy offers superior properties to the elements from which it has been made. Some of these properties will be discussed later.

GRAIN STRUCTURE

The internal structure of almost all metals is granular, that is made up of grains. As a molten metal cools solid crystals begin to form and grow, dependent upon the cooling rate. The final shape, or morphology, of the grains dictates the properties of the metal. Metals with a grain morphology that is rounded have good tensile and compressive properties in all directions, whereas elongated grains may cause the metal to be strong in one direction but weak at right angles to it. The ideal microstructure for most applications is equiaxed, that is grains with similar dimensions in all directions.

STRESS AND STRAIN

Although these terms are widely, and incorrectly, used in everyday life they have very specific meanings when discussing the properties of metals and materials. The definition of stress is load divided by cross-sectional area, thus in a simple example a piece of metal 1cm square subjected to a load of 1 tonne will be more highly stressed than a piece of the same metal 1m square subjected to the same load. The strength of a metal is the stress that it can sustain before fracturing.

Strain is a measurement of the deformation of a metal as the result of stress. In a tensile test it is expressed as the change in length divided by the original length of the test specimen.

HARDNESS AND STRENGTH

There is a direct relationship between these two – an increase in hardness will always result in a strength increase. There may also be a reduction in ductility, which we will come to later. There are several ways of increasing hardness and strength, dependent upon the alloy type. Heat treatment – hardening by rapid cooling (quenching) from high temperature followed by tempering, quenching from a lower temperature – is widely used in steels but has no effect on the 300 series stainless steels that are not hardenable by heat treatment. In many metals the same treatment results in almost the opposite effect: for example, heating copper and many other metals to red heat followed by quenching in water is known as annealing, a process used to soften the metal by eliminating work hardening effects.

The strength of metals is measured in one of two ways: ultimate tensile strength (UTS) or yield strength (YS). When a metal sample is pulled in a tensile test machine it initially deforms elastically, that is it returns to the same shape when the stress is removed. Beyond the yield point it begins to deform plastically, so does not return to the same shape when the stress is removed. The point at which elastic gives way to plastic deformation is the yield strength. As the stress applied in the tensile test continues the strength of the metal increases due to strain hardening, a

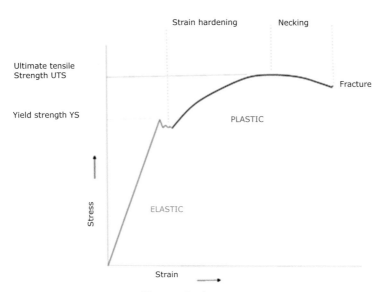

Stress strain curve.

property that will be encountered later in the form of cold working. A further increase in stress causes the sample to break, the highest value recorded before fracture being the UTS. For all metals the UTS will be higher than the YS but in very ductile metals, such as wrought iron and mild steels, the final break strength is lower than the UTS because the cross-sectional area reduces by necking.

The basic unit of strength in metals according to the metric Systeme International (SI) is the Pascal, which is the stress exerted by 1 Newton acting upon 1 square metre of the material. Since a force of 1 Newton is roughly the same as the weight of a small apple, the Pascal is clearly a very low figure, so for convenience the megaPascal (MPa), a million times higher, is normally used. Some typical strengths of metals are shown in the table below, in both SI units and traditional imperial ones.

In the stress versus strain plot for mild steel shown above, the yield strength is easily measured – the point at which the elastic part of the trace gives way to the plastic, known as the yield point, is clearly defined. In most other metals the obvious

Comparison of metal strengths

Metal	Yield strength (MPa)	YS (tons/sq in)	Ultimate tensile strength (MPa)	UTS (tons/sq in)
Mild steel	250	16	400–500	25.9–32
Heat-treated alloy steel	650	42	800	52
Copper	70	4.5	200	13
Brass	200	13	500	32
Cast iron	130	8.4	200	13
Aluminium	95	6.1	110	7.1
Stainless steel	215	13.9	500	32

yield point does not occur, plastic deformation continuing onwards from elastic in a smooth transition. For these metals the YS is measured by drawing a line parallel to the elastic trace from a point corresponding to 0.2 per cent of plastic deformation. The value is known as the 0.2 per cent proof stress.

Hardness Measurement

Hardness of metals is measured by pressing a ball or diamond indenter into the surface and measuring the diameter of the indentation. In industry, measurements may be achieved by one of three methods, Brinell (HB), Vickers (HV) or Rockwell. The first two are quite similar in value whereas Rockwell is very different.

Any metal that has been strengthened, by any of the methods discussed, will have a grain structure that will be destroyed by heating to high temperature. Welding a hardened and tempered steel will anneal it, converting it from a high- or medium-strength material to a soft one. Similarly a cold-worked stainless steel rigging cable or fitting should not be heated to red heat.

DIY Hardness Testing

Occasionally the boat owner might need to measure the hardness, and therefore strength, to determine the properties of a piece of metal. Anchor shanks are a particular example that has come up recently. A laboratory will do it, for a price, but a simpler method is compare it with something of known hardness, perhaps the most likely being a bolt. Grade 8.8 bolts used in construction and automotive industries are widely available from many suppliers.

To carry out the test it is easiest to use only the head of the bolt. The shank can be cut off with a hacksaw, and then the head filed flat. Powered grinders or abrasive cutters should not be used as the heat generated may change the hardness of the bolt.

In the Brinell test a small ball bearing is pressed into the surface of the test metal, where it produces an indent. In the standard test the diameter of the indent is measured and the hardness is determined from tables. In the comparative DIY test two indents are produced using the same load, one in the specimen and one in a metal of known hardness, allowing the diameters to be compared. Ball bearings are considerably harder than the test metals. A ball of 5 or 6mm diameter is used, readily available from cycle shops, for example. The load is applied using a vice, sandwiching the ball between the bolt

Hardness and strength comparison

Approx. tensile strength (MPa)	Brinell hardness (HB)	Vickers hardness (HV)	Rockwell
373	103	108	
472	128	133	
567	156	161	1
693	201	206	15
787	229	234	20
1040	302	310	31
1212	352	369	37
1386	401	424	42
1590	461	501	48

head and the anchor shank. The photographs show a cut sample but an anchor shank, for example, could be used almost as easily, in which case a small area of galvanizing needs to be ground off. It is easier to grease the ball to hold it in place. Neither the exact load nor the ball size is critical. A suitable force is generated by leaning fairly heavily on the vice handle and leaving the load on for about 10 seconds.

The photographs show a comparative test using the head of a metric 8.8 bolt as the standard to evaluate the hardness of an anchor shank that is believed to have a strength of about 800MPa.

The first photograph shows the bolt head, ball and specimen between the vice jaws while the second shows that the indents in the bolt head and specimen are similar in size.

The blue arrows on the right in the third photograph show the indents produced on the shank and bolt head. These are of similar size, as would be expected. On the left, red arrows are the indents produced in the bolt head and a mild steel spacer that has a tensile strength of about 420 MPa. The indent produced in the spacer is obviously larger, signifying softer steel. The ball bearing used is shown at the right.

Hardness testing – comparing the indents made by a ball bearing on a bolt head and the specimen shank.

Hardness testing in a vice.

Hardness testing – comparing the indents made by a ball bearing on a shank and a spacer.

WORK HARDENING (STRAIN HARDENING)

'Work' in this context means plastic deformation such that the grains of which the metal is formed are distorted, which increases their strength. Many items on boats are made from stainless steel to take advantage of its good resistance to corrosion. Unfortunately the most-used alloys, in the 300 series, are not hardenable by heat treatment. In order to increase their strength, items such as shroud wire, rigging fittings, some shackles and other items are work hardened during manufacture by extrusion, stamping or cold rolling. For example, shroud wires are cold drawn through a die that reduces their cross-section, increasing their strength considerably. For 316 stainless steel the strength is doubled by a cold reduction of 40–50 per cent.

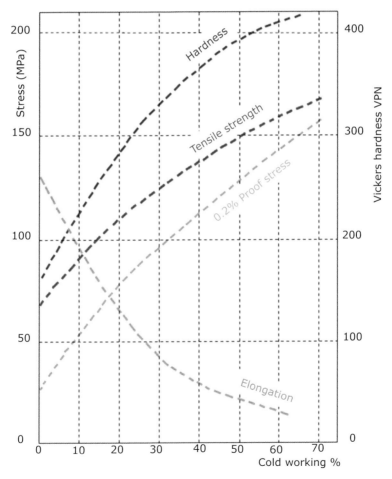

Graph showing the effects of cold working.

DUCTILITY AND BRITTLENESS

Ductile metals deform plastically when loads above the YS are applied. This is a desirable property in most engineering materials, as they can be designed to accept the forces applied to them without fracturing. The opposite of ductility is brittleness, an undesirable property in the vast majority of instances. Shock loads applied to ductile materials, for example an aluminium fitting, result only in some bending or distortion, whereas the same force applied to a brittle material, for example glass or cast iron, results in fracture.

A consequence of increasing strength in most metals is that their ductility reduces, ultimately to a point that they become difficult to use. A good example is steel bolts, such as would be used for a variety of purposes in general engineering. The lowest grade, used for a wide range of duties, might be a Class 4.6, where the first figure is the strength in MPa, 400, and the second is the proportion of the YS to the UTS, 60 per cent. This is a very ductile mild steel. Bolts used for many construction purposes are Class 8.8, 800MPa with YS 80 per cent of this figure, a heat-treated medium carbon steel. Very high-strength bolts made from heat-treated alloy steel are Class 12.9, 1200MPa with YS 90 per cent of this figure. Such bolts need to be used with great care as it is easy to break them by over-tensioning.

Bolt strength and ductility

Bolt class	Strength UTS	Ductility guide YS/UTS
4.6	400MPa	60%
8.8	800MPa	80%
12.9	1200MPa	90%

PRODUCTION METHODS

Metal items are produced by a wide variety of methods, for reasons of economy, cost, strength, other engineering properties and quality of finish.

Casting
Metal in the molten state is poured into a mould that may be formed in a special grade of sand (sand cast) or into a metal mould (die cast). Sand casting is a relatively low-cost manufacturing method as it requires little investment in expensive equipment. Die casting is more expensive due to the cost of manufacturing the die, which in some cases can be a large, complex piece of equipment. For this reason die casting and its more expensive sibling, pressure die casting, are reserved for long production runs in, for example, the automotive industry. In boats sand casting is used for iron keels, although in older boats many bronze items were cast. Many smaller aluminium fittings such as cleats and fairleads are cast – in sand moulds in the majority of cases, though more numerous articles such as cleats and fairleads may be die cast.

Forging
Forging is a process in which hot metal is hammered into shape, as by a blacksmith. Its great advantage is that with skilled design of the dies used and the procedures followed, strength of the finished component can be greatly enhanced, in a rather similar way that grain in wood gives strength in the preferred direction of loading.

Stamping
Small parts in a variety of metal alloys are produced by stamping, either hot or cold. Hot stamping is used where the alloy

is brittle at room temperature or to take advantage of particular metallurgical factors. Cold stamping of ductile metals may be used to work harden the final article, a particularly useful technique where heat treatment cannot be used, such as with austenitic stainless steels.

Hot and Cold Rolling

Steel and many non-ferrous metals are hot rolled to produce bar, plate, strip and angle sections. The energy required to deform metals at higher temperatures is reduced, the metals are not work hardened and grain structures may be enhanced. Most industrial steel is produced by hot rolling.

Where close sizes, good finish and accurate control of properties are required in wire, sheet and angle sections the normal production method is cold rolling. The energy input is high, resulting in increases of strength due to work hardening, but annealing may be needed between passes to remove these effects.

Extrusion

Pipe and tubing is produced by a process in which nearly molten metal is forced through an annular die at high pressure. Copper pipe is perhaps the most well-known example of this production method. Hollow sections in steel are produced by hot rolling and folding to shape, the edges being resistance welded to close them into a tube.

Fabrication

Very many products are made today by welding plate and other sections together to form a complex shape. Although carbon steel is the most common metal used, many aluminium, stainless steel and copper alloy articles are made in the same way.

STANDARDS

A vast range of standards exists for every type of metal, resulting in very confusing designations for the user. In the past each major country issued their own national standards but in Europe these are gradually being amalgamated into European Norms (EN). USA standards differ from these. I have used the British nomenclature of BS970 for metals throughout the book, as this is the system widely used and understood by boat builders and users. However, it is not unusual to see metals described by UK manufacturers using the old standards that preceded BS970, for example En58 stainless steel and En19 alloy steel. It is far beyond the scope of this book to give equivalent standards for all of these – indeed a reference book I used years ago ran to over 2,000 pages. However, the internet will usually find any equivalents that may be required.

The BS970 code number is constructed as follows.

The first three symbols are a number code indicating the type of steel:

000–199	Carbon and carbon-manganese steels. The number represents the manganese content × 100
200–240	Free cutting steels. The second and third number indicate the sulphur content × 100
250	Silicon-manganese valve steels
300–499	Stainless and heat-resisting steels
500–999	Alloy steels

The fourth symbol is a letter code:

A	The steel is supplied to a chemical composition
H	The steel is supplied to a harden-ability specification
M	The steel is supplied to a mechanical property specification
S	The steel is a stainless steel

The fifth and sixth symbol is a number that is the actual mean carbon content × 100.

For example the steels used for the majority of chain sold in UK to Grade 30 or 40 are to BS970 040A08 or BS970 070M20, respectively. Grade 30 chain steel has a manganese content of 0.40, is supplied to composition only with no requirement for a strength specification and has a carbon content of 0.04 per cent. The steel for Grade 40 steel has higher manganese and carbon contents and is required to have a minimum tensile strength. In practice the specification allows a range of compositions, thus the manganese and carbon figures tend to lie at the middle of the allowable range.

ELEMENT SYMBOLS

Throughout the book I have used conventional symbols for the elemental metals being discussed. The ones used (as well as other common elements) are shown in the table below.

Chemical elements and their symbols

Symbol	Element	Symbol	Element
As	Arsenic	Mn	Manganese
Au	Gold	Mo	Molybdenum
B	Boron	N	Nitrogen
Be	Beryllium	Na	Sodium
Bi	Bismuth	Nb	Niobium
C	Carbon	Ni	Nickel
Ca	Calcium	O	Oxygen
Cd	Cadmium	P	Phosphorus
Cl	Chlorine	Pb	Lead
Co	Cobalt	Pt	Platinum
Cr	Chromium	S	Sulphur
Cu	Copper	Sb	Antimony
Fe	Iron	Si	Silicon
H	Hydrogen	Sn	Tin
Hg	Mercury	Ti	Titanium
In	Indium	V	Vanadium
K	Potassium	W	Tungsten
Li	Lithium	Zn	Zinc
Mg	Magnesium	Zr	Zirconium

CHAPTER 2

Iron and Steel

Iron (Fe) is an element that, in common with most other pure metals, has very poor engineering properties. Nevertheless it has many uses in the form of Armco iron, not least as crash barriers, where its high ductility absorbs impact effectively, but also as magnets and in specialist electrical applications as ferrite, the phase formed in iron containing very little carbon.

In by far the majority of applications iron is used in combination with other elements, primarily carbon but with many others too. Steels with a carbon content of around 0.1–0.25 per cent and with very low levels of other alloying elements are referred to as 'mild steel', a widely used material that is not hardenable by heat treatment.

The Alloy Steels Research Committee definition states: 'Carbon steels are regarded as steels containing no more than 0.5 per cent manganese and 0.5 per cent silicon, all other steels being regarded as alloy steels.'

Medium-carbon steels contain about 0.30–0.60 per cent carbon. Their chief use is as engineering steels in combination with many other elements but particularly chromium, nickel, molybdenum and vanadium. Engineering steels are used in a wide range of applications where higher strength is required, for example in automotive components such as suspension and engine parts, industrial forgings and many large parts.

High-carbon steels may have carbon contents between about 0.70 and 2.5 per cent and a wide range of alloying elements. They have high strength and wear resistance but ductility and toughness are low, making them suitable for machining tools, drills, rolling element bearings and some fastenings.

Iron with even higher carbon contents, usually 2.5–4.0 per cent, is primarily used for castings and is therefore known as cast iron. In this material much of the carbon separates as graphite flakes, which gives the iron poor tensile properties and brittleness. When this very common type of iron breaks the appearance of the fracture face appears grey and it is thus known as grey cast iron. Its most common alloying element is silicon, added at various levels to refine the size and shape of the graphite flakes.

The image overleaf shows the phases formed between iron and carbon. At room temperature ferrite exists only where no carbon is present, that is pure Fe. Increasing amounts of carbon then form the compound cementite, Fe_3C, that exists as a mixture with ferrite, Fe, the mixture being known as pearlite due to the lamellar appearance of the microstructure. Pearlite in the annealed state is transformed to martensite by heating to above a temperature of 723ºC, by which the carbon is dissolved to form a γ phase known as

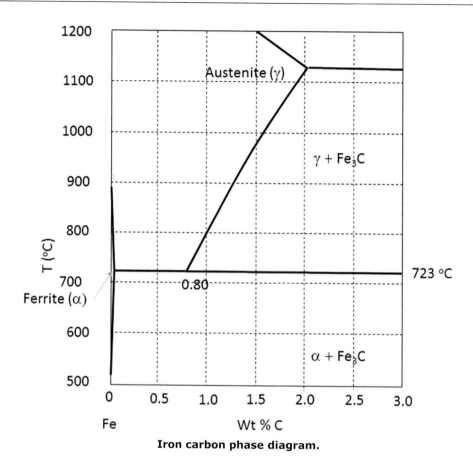

Iron carbon phase diagram.

austenite. The carbon content in the steel needs to be above 0.23 per cent for any useful transformation to take place and thus most engineering steels will contain at least 0.30 per cent of carbon. Rapid cooling by quenching in water or oil causes the austenite to be transformed to martensite, a hard material that is considerably stronger than pearlite but is generally too brittle for use. Tempering, a process of heating to a temperature between about 300 and 600ºC followed by quenching, has the effect of reducing the strength of martensite somewhat but increasing its ductility and toughness. Additions of other metals such as chro-

mium, nickel, manganese, molybdenum, vanadium, silicon and cobalt improve the properties of the alloy by a variety of effects, producing engineering steels that are strong, ductile and tough. The same treatments are applicable to 400 series stainless steels, which are produced in ferritic and martensitic forms.

At carbon contents above about 2.5 per cent some of it begins to separate as graphite flakes in addition to the ferrite and cementite. This separation is largely determined by the amount of silicon present – high silicon favours separation while in low silicon irons more carbon is in the combined state.

All irons and steels have poor corrosion resistance, needing protection from attack by seawater by a wide range of methods such as galvanizing, coatings and anodes.

MILD STEELS

By far the largest use of mild steel on boats is for anchor chain and anchors. Several standards organizations, for example Germanischer-Lloyd, limit the carbon and alloying element content of anchoring equipment in order to reduce the possibility of brittleness in these critical items of equipment. This figure is roughly in line with the transition from mild to medium carbon steels and few items of anchoring equipment will have a carbon content higher than about 0.22 per cent.

Chain

The vast majority of chain sold by chandlers in Europe today is made in China. Isolated manufacture of chain in the typical leisure marine sizes of 6–12mm continues in a few western European countries, most notably by one manufacturer in Italy. Some is also made in Eastern Europe and some in Turkey, but little of this production seems to reach the west. There are several manufacturers based in USA and Canada but even here it is gradually being found that importing offers considerable economic benefits. Whereas at one time Chinese chain was considered to be of poor quality I have been told by a major UK importer that some Chinese chain is now the best available, made on the most modern machinery. Unfortunately this may not hold true for all Chinese production.

Chain production starts with the base wire. As the table below shows, the composition of Grade 30 steel calls for very low carbon and a little manganese, incorporated to avoid the possibility of brittle fracture at low temperature. My assumption is that this would be a relatively expensive steel to produce in China, where the vast majority of steel is refined for constructional steels close to Grade 40 specification. My findings have been that Grade 30 chain made in China is as strong as Grade 40, almost certainly due to its higher carbon content.

Production is entirely automated. Wire is fed into the production machine, where it is cropped to length and the ends of each link are bent into shape around the preceding link, forming the chain. In the next stage the narrow gap between the adjacent link ends is pressed together while an electric current is passed, known as resistance welding. The weld may be wiped immediately afterwards, removing any excess metal. Completed lengths of chain are proof tested about a metre at a time while still in the machine, to a stress of about 200 per cent of the working load limit, WLL. The WLL is normally one-quarter, 25 per cent, of the minimum break load (MBL). Heat-treated chains are quenched and tempered in a continuous process.

From the production machine marine chain passes immediately to the galvanizing plant, where it is first dipped in a caustic solution for degreasing, followed by water washing. It is next pickled in hydrochloric acid for removal of any surface impurities, followed again by water washing. Next it passes into flux that improves the galvanizing process by allowing the molten zinc to fully flow over all surfaces. The flux is dried before the chain finally passes into the zinc bath at a temperature of about 460°C. It remains there until the temperature of the chain reaches that of the zinc, allowing a series of zinc/iron intermetallic compounds to be formed on the surface. The chain may be shaken or centrifuged to remove excess zinc.

Comparison of different grades of carbon steel chain

	Grade 30	Grade 40/43	Grade 70
Composition (% present)			
Iron	Balance	Balance	Balance
Carbon	0.08	0.17–0.23	0.17–0.23
Manganese	0.6 max.	0.7–1.4	0.7–1.4
Phosphorus	0.035 max.	0.05 max.	0.05 max.
Sulphur	0.04	0.05 max.	0.05 max.
Quench/temper			875/600°C
Tensile strength	302–357MPa	550MPa	550–700MPa

Composition of Carbon Steels
for Chain Manufacture
The strength of the finished chain is determined by the composition and treatment of the steel used for its manufacture. Marine chain with the lowest strength is Grade 30, made from low carbon steel such as 040A04 (UK) or SAE 1008 (US). For Grade 40 the carbon and manganese contents are increased, giving about a 25 per cent increase in strength, but without heat treatment. This steel is typically 070M20 (UK) or SAE 1022 (US). Grade 70 chain is manufactured from the same steel as Grade 40 but it is heat treated to increase strength by a further 20 per cent.

Users may derive considerable benefit from changing from a lower grade chain of one size to a stronger grade in a size smaller. The weight of chain being carried can be reduced considerably, typi-cally 100kg when changing from 10mm to 8mm, with no reduction, and often a considerable increase, in strength. The main disadvantage in doing this is that the windlass gypsy needs to be changed, often an expensive modification. However, many long-distance cruisers are making this change, perhaps in parallel with an upgrade in windlass design.

Chain Dimensions
Leisure vessels in most cases carry chain of between 6mm and 12mm wire diameter. Chain is manufactured to a wide range of specifications, dependent

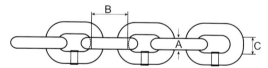

Chain dimensions.

European metric chain sizes and strengths
Grade 30

Wire size	A	B	C	WLL, kN (tons)	MBL, kN (tons)	Weight (kg/m)	Standard
6	6	18.5	8	4 (0.4)	16 (1.6)	0.85	DIN 766 and ISO4565
7					24.4 (2.44)	1.1	DIN 766 and ISO4565
8	8	24	12	7.5 (0.75)	30 (3.0)	1.45	DIN 766 and ISO4565
10	10	28	14	12.5 (1.25)	50 (5.0)	2.3	DIN 766
10	10	30	14	12.5 (1.25)	50 (5.0)	2.3	ISO4565
12	12	36	18	17.5 (1.75)	70 (7.0)	3.8	DIN 766 and ISO4565

Grade 40

Wire size	A	B	C	WLL, kN (tons)	MBL, kN (tons)	Standard
6	6	18.5	9	6.75 (0.675)	27 (2.7)	DIN 766 and ISO4565
7				7.75 (0.775)	31 (3.1)	DIN 766 and ISO4565
8	8	24	10.5	10 (1.0)	40 (4.0)	DIN 766 and ISO4565
10	10	28	14	12.5 (1.25)	50 (5.0)	DIN 766
10	10	30	12	15.5 (1.55)	62 (6.2)	ISO4565
12	12	36	15	22.5 (2.25)	90 (9.0)	DIN 766 and ISO4565

Grade 70

Wire size	A	B	C	WLL, kN (tons)	MBL, kN (tons)	Standard
8	8	24		14 (1.4)	70 (7.0)	DIN 766 and ISO4565
10	10	28		22 (2.2)	110 (11.0)	DIN 766
10	10	30		22 (2.2)	110 (11.0)	ISO4565
12	12	36		31.6 (3.16)	158 (15.8)	DIN 766 and ISO4565

American chain sizes and strengths

USA G30 Proof Coil

Wire size (in)	A (mm)	B (mm)	C (mm)	SWL, kN (lb)	UTS, kN (tons)	Standard
3/16	5.5	24.6	10	3.56 (800)	14.24 (1.42)	ISO G30
1/4	7	25.4	12.7	5.78 (1300)	23.12 (2.32)	ISO G30
5/16	8.4	28.5	12.7	8.45 (1900)	33.8 (3.39)	ISO G30
3/8	10	31	15.8	11.79 (2650)	47.16 (4.73)	ISO G30
1/2	13	38	20.6	20.02 (4500)	80.08 (8.04)	ISO G30

USA G43 High test

Wire size (in)	A (mm)	B (mm)	C (mm)	SWL, kN (lb)	UTS, kN (tons)	Standard
1/4	7	21.3	10.41	11.57 (2600)	46.28 (4.64)	ISO G43
5/16	8.4	26.2	12.95	17.35 (3900)	69.4 (6.96)	ISO G43
3/8	10	31	15.0	24.02 (5400)	96.08 (9.64)	ISO G43
7/16	11.8	35.6	16.5	32.03 (7200)	128.12 (12.86)	ISO G43
1/2	13	40.34	19.3	40.92 (9200)	163.68 (16.43)	ISO G43

Grade 30 BBB (all dimensions inches)

Chain size	Wire diameter	Inner L	Inner W	Outer L	Outer W	Links/ft
1/4	0.281	0.87	0.43	1.43	0.99	14
5/16	0.343	1.00	0.50	1.691	1.19	12
3/8	0.406	1.09	0.62	1.901	1.43	11
1/2	0.531	1.34	0.75	2.401	1.81	9

Grade 40 BBB (all dimensions inches)

Chain size	Wire diameter	Inner L	Inner W	Outer L	Outer W	Links/ft
1/4	0.274	0.845	0.41	1.39	0.96	14.2
5/16	0.330	1.03	0.50	1.69	1.16	11.7
3/8	0.394	1.22	0.60	2.01	1.39	9.8
7/16	0.467	1.40	0.66	2.33	1.59	8.6
1/2	0.510	1.59	0.77	2.61	1.79	7.6

upon the intended duty. Stronger chains than the common marine grades shown here are made but these are not galvanized due to the risk of hydrogen-induced cracking (HIC), which can be a problem in high-strength steels. Chain made to metric and imperial dimensions differs considerably, as shown in these tables. Although strength is measured in kiloNewtons (kN) according to the SI method it is common for chain strength to be quoted in tons force, which is approximately a tenth of the value in kN.

Few users have facilities for testing potential chain purchases but I have devised a simple test that requires only one link of chain and gives useful information regarding the quality of the weld and adhesion of the galvanizing. The single link is cut with a hacksaw on the long side opposite to the weld. The link is held in a vice with the weld down. An adjustable spanner is used to bend the link to about 90 degrees. A well-made weld will easily take this treatment whereas a weld with poor penetration will crack. Tensile testing

DIY chain test in a vice. The final link of the sample chain is cut on the side opposite the weld and clamped in a vice with the weld down. An adjustable spanner is used to bend the link, which is achieved easily with the ductile chain steel.

Chain link fracture. The chain from which this link was taken failed to achieve its required strength in a tensile test. The DIY test confirmed the poor quality of the weld.

Brittle fractures. The arrow points to the fracture that occurred in the tensile testing machine. The straight fracture with very little plastic deformation is characteristic of a brittle fracture. The link at the left fractured in a similar manner in the bend test.

Flaked galvanizing. Zinc galvanizing flaked off the link in this test. Correctly applied galvanizing will survive such bending without losing adhesion.

of chain with this defect typically results in strengths of half or less than specification. At the same time, well-bonded galvanizing will remain adhered to the link, whereas poorly applied galvanizing will flake off.

Anchors

Historic Types

For hundreds of years traditional designs of anchor were manufactured from wrought iron made by the puddling process. Pig iron direct from the blast furnace was melted with millscale and iron oxide, causing the impurities to form a slag largely composed of iron silicate. The freezing point of the metal was increased by this process and the metal solidified in the furnace to a pasty mass of metal mixed with large amounts of slag. The mixture was removed from the furnace and hammered into rough bars. In turn these were piled and folded together, heated and rolled into sections. The slag is thus elongated into fibres that strengthen the metal in the longitudinal direction. The resulting metal can have improved corrosion resistance and the ability to resist shock loading.

Chain was also made using the same techniques from at least 1800 onwards. The famous photograph of Isambard Kingdom Brunel during construction of the Great Eastern shows him standing by wrought iron chain.

Two ship's anchors made in wrought iron. The traditional form (Admiralty pattern or Fisherman) has two flukes, a shank and a stock that is longer than the flukes. The anchor nearer to the camera is a stockless type that stows more easily.

CQR

Until the 1930s there was little choice for the yachtsman when it came to purchasing an anchor, the Fisherman being just about the only type available. In 1933, mathematician and physicist Sir Geoffrey Ingram Taylor, a professor at Trinity College, Cambridge, invented the CQR anchor. *Yachting Monthly* published his paper, 'The Holding Power of Anchors', in April 1934. Although a keen yachtsman himself, his anchor research was directed at flying boats, which needed anchors with minimum weight and high holding. His intention was that his new design would be named the 'Secure' but this was deemed by the patent office to be a word in common usage and it was refused. It was therefore named the CQR instead.

The CQR is manufactured by drop forging, that is, hammering semi-molten metal into its final shape in a die using a mechanical hammer. The dies used in drop forging may be 'open' or 'closed'; in the case of the CQR they are closed, accounting for the raised lettering on each side of the shank. Drop forging produces a fibrous structure that, when expertly made, offers considerable enhancement of the metal's strength. The fluke is made in the same way, the heavy tip section being steel throughout, unlike some other designs that have lead in the tip for additional weight. The two sections are connected together via a hinge that allows the fluke to rotate into the seabed.

Some models of the CQR have been manufactured by casting. These can be identified by the marked weight, which is shown as a number plus ½, whereas the weight of forged anchors is marked as a whole number.

CQR Copies

Innumerable copies of the CQR have been produced, some made by sound engineering methods, others less so. The genuine article is one of the most expensive anchors in the marketplace, thanks to its manufacturing technique. Shortcuts have clearly been made in anchors costing a quarter of the price of the genuine one. In a recent brief survey carried out in an east coast marina I counted almost twenty CQR copies, some cast, some fabricated but none drop forged as far as I could tell.

Danforth

The Danforth anchor was invented by American Richard Danforth in the 1940s for use aboard landing craft. Its appearance is reminiscent of the stockless type with a rectangular section shank and two hinged flat triangular flukes. This relatively low-tech anchor is manufactured by fabrication from stock material and is widely copied throughout the world.

Bruce

Although genuine Bruce anchors for the leisure market have not been made for many years, their far larger siblings are still manufactured and in daily use in the offshore oil industry, where they moor exploration and production rigs. The leisure version was designed in the 1970s and has been manufactured in the UK, Belgium and Brazil in low-carbon cast steel. Carbon is the principal alloying element in these steels but other elements are present in small quantities, including silicon from 0.25 to 0.80 per cent and manganese from 0.50 per cent to 1.00 per cent. Small amounts of aluminium may be added as a deoxidant.

Additional alloying elements may be added to improve the properties of the product. These can include nickel (0.5 per cent), chromium (0.25 per cent), molybdenum (0.10 per cent) and vanadium (0.05 per cent).

Cast steels are stronger and tougher than cast irons but are more difficult to produce. Heat treatment may be required to ensure the preferred microstructure of small, equiaxed grains.

Bruce Copies

Unfortunately it has proved very easy for other manufacturers to make copies of cast anchors, which has resulted in the

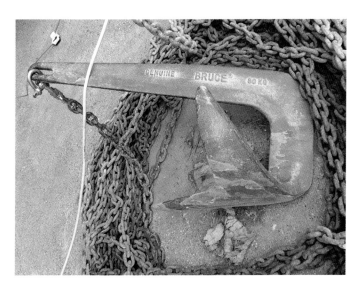

An elderly, large Bruce anchor made in the UK.

A later Bruce anchor, made in Belgium.

appearance on the market of some very poor examples, apparently made either of cast iron or from scrap steel with very poor metallurgical control. Many of these copies have proved to be brittle, fracturing at relatively light loadings.

The photograph of a failed low-cost Bruce copy, shows several interesting features. First, corrosion on the left side indicates that the crack had been growing for some considerable time. Second, the grains at the lower part of the final bright fracture are long and normal to the surface, known as columnar, whereas those at the top are equiaxed, or regular in shape. This structure indicates poor control of cooling rate on manufacture and is unacceptable in any component required to resist stress.

Fabricated Anchors
Since the 1980s the vast majority of anchors have been manufactured by fabrication methods, that is, welded construction using cut plate. Examples include Delta, Bugel, Spade, Rocna and Manson among many others.

Flukes are typically made in mild steel with relatively low strength, around 250–270MPa. Although one or two designs

The shank of an anchor that failed in very light loading, wind strength around force three. The anchor was a low-cost copy of a Bruce. IONA OF FIFE

have been manufactured using a combination of cast and fabricated construction the majority of current anchors are entirely made using welded plate. Modern design emphasis on tip weight dictates that shanks be made as light as possible, which of course has an effect on their strength. There seems to be general agreement that a yield strength of about 700MPa is required to resist lateral bending in shanks made from cut plate. Several alternative methods are employed to provide lightweight but strong shanks, including plate materials made from heat-treatable steels and three-dimensional shapes. Some innovative solutions have been found.

One of the first fabricated anchors to be marketed in the UK was the Delta, a rigid plough anchor that soon achieved great popularity that continues to this day. The anchor was developed from the CQR by Simpson-Lawrence in 1992, now marketed by Lewmar. Deltas are made in both galvanized steel and stainless steel versions (the stainless steel one will be described later). Lewmar tell me that the shank of the galvanized steel version is made from an alloy steel of their own specification, typically to BS EN 10113-S460N, with a yield strength of 600–720MPa. The ballast tip is either cast or forged, 070M20, A1 grade, with a tensile strength 440MPa. The main part of the fluke is cut from plate, and then folded in three planes. This is subsequently welded to two other parts to form the ballast assembly. The anchors are proof loaded prior to galvanizing.

The anchors are finally hot dip galvanized to BS729/EN1461.

Bugel
Rolf Kaczirek, a German circumnavigator, invented the Bugel anchor in the 1980s. This could be said to be the forerunner of new generation anchor design, moving away from the plough to a flat fluke design and adding a roll bar to ensure that it would always self-right on the seabed. It seems that the design was not patented and plans are available for anybody to make it. The best-known commercial manufacturer is WASI & Co. in Wuppertal, Germany. The anchor is totally fabricated

Delta steel compositions BS EN 10113-S460N (%)

C	Si	Mn	S	P	Nb	V	Al	Ti	Cr	Ni	Mo	Cu	N
0.20	0.60	1.0–1.6	0.30	0.35	0.05	0.20	0.02	0.03	0.30	0.80	0.10	0.70	0.025

070M20 (%)

	C	Si	Mn	S	P	Cr	Ni	Mo
Min.	0.16	0.10	0.50					
Max.	0.24	0.40	0.90	0.05	0.05	0.30	0.40	0.15

Mechanical properties of 070M20

Material	Yield (MPa)	UTS (MPa)	Elongation (%)	Hardness (HB)
Min.	215	430	21	126
Max.				179

from plate material of different thicknesses, available in galvanized steel and stainless steel.

New Generation Anchors

The shanks of Spade anchors are made in a triangular hollow section, a complex fabrication method that has resulted in tip weight being a massive 50 per cent of the total anchor weight. Shanks made using this technique are strong and light, but this is an expensive and time-consuming production method.

Both Rocna and Manson have selected high-strength steels for use in plate shanks, reducing production time at the expense of more costly material. Limitations in the allowable carbon content of anchoring equipment have caused both companies to find solutions outside the use of medium-carbon alloy steels. For the shanks of their Supreme model, and possibly others, Manson use Bisplate 80 steel, a low-carbon, low-alloy steel with very small additions of boron.

Shanks of original Rocna anchors made in New Zealand were also made in Bisplate 80. Following the purchase of the company by Canada Metal (Pacific) the shank material was changed. I carried out a thorough test programme on a new anchor for *Yachting Monthly* magazine and found as follows:

This composition is typical of high-strength, low-alloy (HSLA) steel, a modern engineering steel widely used at relatively low cost due to the small content of expensive and scarce alloying elements. HSLA steels are used in cars, trucks, cranes, bridges and other structures that require a good strength-to-weight ratio. HSLA steels are usually 20–30 per cent lighter than a carbon steel with the same strength. They may also be more resistant to corrosion than conventional steels thanks to the absence of pearlite.

These results showed the mechanical strength of the latest version of the anchor to be slightly lower than those made with the original Bisplate 80, although fully acceptable.

Mantus anchors are a more recent addition to the field. Their overall appearance is similar to the Rocna in that they have concave flukes, a roll bar and are fabricated from plate. When first introduced in about 2011 the shank material was A36 mild steel, a design choice that attracted con-

Composition of Bisplate 80 (%)

Section (mm)	C	P	Mn	S	Cr	Mo	B
5<16	0.18	0.025	1.5	0.008	0.25	0.25	0.002
16<80	0.20	0.025	1.5	0.008	0.30	0.25	0.002

Mechanical properties of Bisplate 80

Properties	Specification	Typical
0.2 per cent proof stress	690MPa (min.)	750MPa
Tensile strength	790–930MPa	830MPa
Elongation	18% (min.)	26%
Hardness		255 HB

Composition of a Rocna shank (%)

C	P	Mn	Si	S	Cr	Ni	Mo	B	Nb	V	Cu	Ti
0.08	0.011	1.52	0.23	<0.005	0.03	0.01	<0.01	<0.0005	0.04	<0.01	0.01	0.09

Mechanical properties of a Rocna shank

	Ultimate tensile strength (MPa)	Yield strength (MPa)	Elongation (%)	Charpy value (Joules)	Vickers hardness (HV)
Anchor	742	677	25.5	93	258, 254, 253

Chemical composition of A514 (%), as used for Mantus shanks

	C	Mn	P	S	Si	Cr	Mo	V	B
Min.	0.12	0.95			0.20	0.40	0.20	0.03	0.0005
Max.	0.21	1.30	0.035	0.008	0.35	0.65	0.30	0.08	0.005

siderable criticism. In 2013 they changed this to A514, an 800MPa steel. Being made in the USA, the Mantus uses steel to ASTM standards.

The shank is bolted to the fluke part using four high-tensile bolts. These are US Grade 5, with dimensions in imperial units of proof load 85,000psi, minimum yield strength 92,000psi and minimum UTS 120,000psi. These strengths convert to 586MPa, 634MPa and 827MPa, respectively, and are very close to metric Class 8.8 values.

ALLOY STEELS

Machinery Components

Many items of machinery exist in the typical yacht, not only the engine but also the gearbox, drive and flexible couplings, constant velocity joints (Aquadrive and others), windlass, bow thruster and other items. In general these parts are made from some type of steel, which, unless lu-

Mechanical properties of A514

0.2% YS (MPa)	Min. UTS (MPa)	Elongation (%)	Reduction of area (min. %)
690	760–895	16	35

bricated inside a casing, need to be coated to provide corrosion resistance. Paint is probably the most common protection but galvanizing is also used.

Mild steel is used throughout the engine, as low-strength nuts and bolts, brackets, couplings and flanges, mountings and bearers. Some fastenings have higher strength requirements and for these an alloy steel is used, its grade invariably marked on the head of the bolt.

Allen-headed bolts may be encountered: if these are black their strength will be high, probably 10.9 or greater, but Allen-headed stainless steel bolts are increasingly used on boats and these are considerably weaker.

Within the engine and gearbox can be found many examples of alloy steels specified where greater strength and durability are required, for shafts, cam followers, tappets, connecting rods and gears. All of these components are heat treated during manufacture, usually requiring a two-stage process of quenching followed by tempering at a specific temperature to produce the required strength. The martensitic structure produced by such treatment would be modified by heating to a temperature above 723°C, so any maintenance activity requiring heating to red heat in order to remove seized parts, or welding for repair, will prevent the part from performing as it should. The engine block, crankcase and cylinder head of most auxiliary engines are made from cast iron, although aluminium cylinder heads are used, particularly in engines originally designed for automobiles.

Most good-quality tools are made from chrome-vanadium steels, including spanners and socket sets requiring strength, toughness and good wear properties.

Metric bolt head markings.

All steels shown other than mild steel are heat treated by quenching and tempering.

Rolling element bearings in machinery are usually made from a heat-treated steel containing 1 per cent carbon and 1 per cent chromium, which makes them very hard and brittle.

Shackles

Galvanized shackles and connectors as sold for leisure marine purposes such as connecting chain to anchors are almost always made from mild steel, with strength of about 250MPa. The quality of some can be surprisingly poor. When a number of chandlery-bought galvanized steel shackles was tested it was found that several 10mm shackles failed at lower force than

Metric bolts

Head marking, class and material	Mechanical properties		
	Proof load (MPa)	Min. yield strength (MPa)	Min. tensile strength (MPa)
Class 8.8 medium carbon steel, quenched and tempered	580	640	800
Class 10.9 alloy steel, quenched and tempered	830	940	1040
Class 12.9 alloy steel, quenched and tempered	970	1100	1220
A2 stainless steel alloy with 17–19% chromium and 8–13% nickel		210 min., 450 typical	500 min., 700 typical

Compositions of various steels (%)

Steel	Duty	C	Si	Mn	Cr	Ni	Mo	V
Mild steel 230M07	General	0.07–0.15	0.10 max.	0.80–1.20				
709M40	Gears, pinions, shafts	0.35–0.45	0.10–0.35	0.50–0.80	0.90–1.50		0.20–0.40	
817M40	Connecting rods, gear shafts	0.35–0.45	0.10–0.35	0.45–0.70	0.50–0.80	1.30–1.80	0.40–0.70	
735A50	Crankshafts, gears, tools	0.45–0.55	0.50 max.	0.50–0.80	0.80–1.20			0.15 min.
080M50	Crankshafts, drills, axes	0.45–0.60	0.10–0.40	0.60–0.80				

Effect of alloying elements in steel

Element	Properties
Carbon (C)	Increases strength
	Increases hardness and improves resistance to wear and abrasion
Chromium (Cr)	Increases hardness, tensile strength and toughness
	Provides resistance to wear and corrosion
Cobalt (Co)	Increases strength and hardness and permits quenching at higher temperatures
	Intensifies the individual effects of other elements in more complex steels
Copper (Cu)	Increases corrosion resistance
	Increases wear resistance
Manganese (Mn)	Increases hardenability, wear resistance and tensile strength
	De-oxidizes and degasifies to remove oxygen from molten metal
	In larger quantities, increases hardness and brittleness
Molybdenum (Mo)	Increases strength, hardness, hardenability and toughness
	Improves machinability and resistance to corrosion
Nickel (Ni)	Adds strength, hardness and corrosion resistance
Phosphorus (P)	Improves strength, machinability and hardness
	Creates brittleness in high concentrations
Silicon (Si)	Increases yield strength
	Increases tensile strength
	De-oxidizes and degasifies to remove oxygen from molten metal
Sulphur (S)	Improves machinability when used in minute quantities
Tungsten (W)	Adds strength, toughness and hardness
Vanadium (V)	Increases strength, hardness and resistance to shock impact
	Retards grain growth

8mm chain. The pin of a 10mm shackle will pass through a link of 8mm chain but larger pins will not.

If greater strength and reliability are required, it is possible to purchase proof-tested shackles from lifting and hoisting specialists, although the higher strength versions are not galvanized to guard against hydrogen-induced cracking. A variety of production methods is used, including carbon steels, heat-treated alloy steels and forged alloy steels. In some cases the proof load is marked on the shackle. The proof load is twice the working load limit (WLL) and half of the minimum break load (MBL), that is a safety factor of 4:1, although some lifting equipment uses a safety factor of 6:1 for alloy steels and 5:1 for carbon steels.

The steels used for shackles are similar to those used for bolts – Grades 6 and 8 for carbon steels, Grade 10 for quenched and tempered alloy steels. Typical alloying elements are chromium, nickel, molybdenum and vanadium.

C-links for joining chain whilst passing through a windlass are made from mild steel unless bought from lifting and hoisting specialists, in which case they are made from heat-treated medium carbon or alloy steel. Heat-treated steels are considerably harder and tougher than mild steel, which is reflected in the difficulty experienced in making up the links. The rivets incorporated in each half need to be peened over on the outside of its opposing half. In mild steels this is easily achieved, giving a warning that the link when made up will be relatively weak. Better grades of C-link are discussed at the end of this chapter.

KEELS

Three main keel constructions are used for yachts today. These are cast iron for most mass-produced yachts; cast lead for some, mainly more up-market yachts; and fabricated steel for small production runs, racing boats and similar vessels. Lead keels will be covered in the section under that metal.

Cast Iron

The greatest use of iron alloys by far, in tonnage terms, is cast iron for keels. Iron is an excellent metal for casting, relatively easy to use and able to form detailed and intricate shapes. Casting is carried out in specialized factories known as foundries, where molten iron is poured into moulds whose shape is formed in sand.

The casting process commences with the creation of a pattern, usually in wood for items that will be produced many times. The specialist sand used to form the shape of the pattern is made by mixing with clay as a bonding agent and moistened with water that strengthens the aggregate and allows it to set once the water has dried out. The sand aggregate is packed around the pattern in mould boxes, together with a

Shackle steel composition (%)

	C	Mn	P max.	S max.	Si
Grade 6	0.3	0.29–1.06	0.025	0.025	0.10 min.
Grade 8	0.28–0.55	0.6	0.035	0.040	0.15–0.35

gate into which the molten metal is poured and risers that allow the air being dispelled, along with any gases created during the process, to exit the mould. Simple moulds, of the type used for keels, are made in two halves, allowing the pattern to be removed once the sand has hardened, but more complex moulds may be made of multiple parts.

Modern keels are cast upright, allowing all gases to be expelled to leave a high-density metal, but some older boat builders cast their keels horizontally. The result can be considerable differences in the condition of the surface from one side to the other, and in the worst cases gas cavities that subsequently corrode unevenly, creating an unusual appearance.

Gas cavities in the keel of a Westerly yacht. The cavities are formed when the casting is made horizontally, making release of the gases more problematic. Similar problems have been reported in keels from several other builders.

The chief constituent of cast iron is pig iron, the iron as it comes from the blast furnace. 'Pig' is the name given to the billets of iron in the solidified state. Modern cast iron production is carried out in electric induction furnaces although in the past it was more commonly done in cupola furnaces, a type of blast furnace using coke for heating. Pig iron is melted with scrap iron and steel, following which the carbon and silicon contents are corrected as necessary, and levels of undesirable elements such as sulphur and phosphorus are reduced. In some grades of cast iron other elements are then added to the melt but this is not typical for keel production. The molten iron is then decanted into a ladle, or sometimes an electrically heated holding furnace, from where it is poured into the moulds.

Grey cast iron is the most commonly used cast iron for all purposes, including keels. Its name derives from its graphitic microstructure, which gives fractures of the material a grey appearance. Most cast irons contain 2.5–4.0 per cent carbon and 1–3 per cent silicon, with the remainder being iron. The free graphite within the cast iron microstructure has little strength, and thus cast iron has poor tensile strength and shock resistance compared with steel, but its compressive strength is reasonable. One beneficial property of the graphite flakes is that they act as stress relievers that arrest fatigue cracks, making the metal largely immune from this problem. The mechanical properties of the alloy are totally dependent upon the size and morphology (shape) of the graphite flakes present in the microstructure. The shape of the product largely determines the cooling rate after casting, which itself determines the final properties. Directional solidification is important in the manufacturing process to ensure that all areas of the casting are able to access liquid metal before they solidify. In some cases, particularly those keels with more complex shapes such as wing keels, certain areas need to solidify at a faster rate. This is done by the use of chills, which are solid metallic shapes that absorb heat and cause the local molten metal to solidify earlier. Chills are of two types, either internal and of the same material as the casting, or external, placed in the mould outside the final casting shape forming the mould itself.

Keel bolts are drilled and tapped after casting to suit the requirements of the boat. Bolt materials today are generally AISI 304 or 316 grade stainless steel although in fairly recent times several manufacturers have used carbon steel bolts. Beneteau and Moody (Marine Projects) are two examples. Many other materials are used, including bronze, Monel and high-strength stainless steels, but the 300 series are the most common today. In most cases the nuts and washers inside the hull are made from carbon steels to avoid the problem of galling between stainless steels in combination.

Fabricated Steel

Steel keels for race boats and other yachts manufactured in small numbers are constructed by the welding of steel plate, usually with a heavy lead torpedo bulb to provide righting moment. Not only is this a cheaper production method for short runs, it results in a keel that is relatively light in the structural part but puts maximum

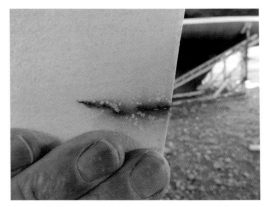

A crack in a keel only a few years old. Fatigue is most unlikely in this material and position, as is any form of stress-corrosion cracking. It is assumed that this is a casting defect, in which solidification occurred prematurely due to interrupted pouring. Seawater penetrated the crack, leading to the corroded appearance.

weight as far as possible from the hull. Bending loads imposed on the steel part during heeling can be very high, requiring complex, three-dimensional construction methods. In some well-publicized cases, such as that of *Hooligan V*, in which Jamie Butcher lost his life, the design intent of the keel designer was compromised by the builder, who omitted certain parts of the internal structure as an aid to construction, but in the majority of yachts in which this method is used it is perfectly reliable.

Properties of grey cast iron

Name	Nominal composition (%)	Tensile strength (MPa)	Elongation (%)	Hardness (HB)	Uses
Grey cast iron ASTM A48	C 3.4, Si 1.8, Mn 0.5	344	0.5	260 HB	Engine blocks, gearbox casings, keels

This type of construction uses hot-rolled structural steels intended for general welding, classified as carbon manganese steels. Additional manganese improves ductility and malleability, particularly at low temperatures where the ductile/brittle transition temperature is lowered.

Weathering steel, usually known by its trade name of Corten, is a steel that is designed to develop a passive corrosion-resistant film in a similar way to stainless steels. It initially corrodes to the familiar orange colour of rust but the black colour of corrosion products on conventional structural steels does not occur.

Corten is used mostly in structural applications but has become popular for steel yacht construction. Perhaps its best-known use is in the construction of the Angel of the North statue outside Gateshead.

Both versions, under specifications ASTM A 242 and ASTM A 588, have yield strengths of 340MPa and UTS of 480MPa in all sizes other than 19–25mm for ASTM A 242, for which the YS is 320MPa and UTS 460MPa.

OTHER CARBON STEEL COMPONENTS

In some cases glass-fibre yachts are strengthened by the inclusion of metal frames to take rigging and rudder loads, often constructed from galvanized steel tubing or other sections. These are typi-

Composition of EN 10025-2:2004, European standard for hot-rolled structural steel – non-alloy structural steels (%)

Type	Carbon	Manganese	Silicon	Phosphorus max.	Sulphur max.	Nitrogen max.	Copper max.
S235JR	0.17	1.40		0.040	0.040	0.012	0.55
S275JR	0.21	1.50		0.040	0.040	0.012	0.55
S335JR	0.24	1.60	0.55	0.040	0.040	0.012	0.55

Mechanical properties of hot-rolled structural steel

Type	Min. YS (MPa)	Min. UTS (MPa)	Min. elongation (%)
S235JR	225–235	360–510	26
S275JR	265–275	410–560	23
S335JR	345–355	470–630	22

Chemical composition of Corten grades (%)

Grade	C	Si	Mn	P	S	Cr	Cu	V	Ni
Corten A	0.12	0.25–0.75	0.20–0.50	0.01–0.20	0.030	0.50–1.25	0.25–0.55		0.65
Corten B	0.16	0.30–0.50	0.80–1.25	0.030	0.030	0.40–0.65	0.25–0.40	0.02–0.10	0.40

cally made from structural steel that has low carbon content for good welding performance. It is important to inspect these structural items periodically, especially in hard-to-reach areas, where corrosion may have taken hold.

The upper rudder bearing support on a Jeanneau Sun Odyssey 45.2. The structure is made from galvanized carbon steel and is difficult to inspect due to being high in the lazarette. This view is the only one available without dismantling the structure.

The top of the housing was impossible to inspect without removing it from the boat. After removal it was found to be severely corroded and total failure was imminent.

End view of bearing housing.

C-Links

C-links are a means of joining chain whilst allowing it to pass through the gypsy of a windlass. Their construction resembles two letter C shapes back to back, the two halves riveted together to strengthen and retain them.

It would be unreasonable to expect C-links made in the same steel as chain of the same wire size to have equal strength with it, although many of the ones sold in the average chandlery are made of almost exactly the same mild steel. My testing has shown many of these to have only around 40 per cent of the strength of chain of the same size. When making them up by peening over the rivets through the holes in the opposing half, the hammer force required is very low as the metal is soft and deforms easily.

C-link. GRAHAM SNOOK

In order to provide equivalent strength to the chain it is necessary to strengthen the C-link by making it from a stronger type of steel. C-links available from lifting and hoisting equipment suppliers, and from companies specializing in these devices, are made using hardened and tempered alloy steels. The rivets in these are considerably more difficult to make up, needing vigorous attention from a heavy hammer. Better examples are as strong as the chain they fit.

CHAPTER 3

Stainless Steels

It may not have hit the headlines, but 2013 marked the centenary of the accidental discovery in 1913 that the corrosion resistance of steel is increased dramatically by the addition of chromium. Since then a wide range of corrosion-resistant steels has been introduced with up to six alloying elements. Several of these are widely used in the leisure boating industry but all can suffer problems under certain conditions.

The fundamental corrosion resistance of these alloys is provided by the chromium, thanks to its ability to create a passive film of chromium oxide upon surfaces exposed to oxygen. Chromium oxide forms in seconds upon freshly machined surfaces when exposed to an environment that can provide the oxygen required, for example air or aerated water. In certain specific conditions the passive layer may not form readily, in which case passivation may be required. Passivation is carried out by pickling in a strong oxidizer, for which nitric acid, citric acid or nitric acid/sodium dichromate solutions are used.

surface of machined surfaces, particularly screw threads, consists of many peaks and troughs when viewed at high magnification. In tribology terms these are known as asperities. When forced together at high pressure these asperities can weld themselves together, making the joint impossible to move. The problem is widely encountered in rigging turnbuckles and bottle-screws but also in nuts and bolts. There is no solution other than cutting the components apart for replacement.

There are several palliatives that assist with preventing the problem. Since the mechanism is welding, the best means of avoiding it is to introduce a substance that contaminates the surface, making welding less likely. The best of these has been found to be molybdenum disulphide, marketed for this purpose by several manufacturers. Copper-containing greases have also been found to be helpful, although perhaps rather less so. Unfortunately oil and grease tend to extrude from the loaded asperities and are not especially beneficial.

GALLING

A problematic property of most stainless steels, but 300 series in particular, is the propensity of highly loaded, close-fitting components to weld themselves together in a process known as galling. The

200 SERIES

The 200 series is little known outside USA. Whereas the 300 series alloys contain about 8 per cent of nickel, in the 200 series this expensive metal is replaced by manganese. The mechanical properties of these

Composition of 200 grade stainless steels

	C (%)	Cr (%)	Mn (%)	Cu (%)	Ni (%)	N (%)	Fe (%)	YS (MPa)	UTS (MPa)	Elongation (%)
201	0.15 max.	17	6.0		4.5	0–0.25	Balance	310 min.	655 min.	40 min.
201L	0.03 max.	17	6.0		4.5	0–0.25	Balance			
202	0.15	18	8.5		5	0.25	Balance			
204Cu	0.15	16	7	2.5	2	0.15	Balance			

alloys are similar to those of the 300 series, with corrosion resistance not quite as good as 316 but equal to 304. The main grades are 201, 201L, 202 and 204. As with the 300 series, these alloys are non-magnetic.

AUSTENITIC (300 SERIES) STAINLESS STEELS

The addition of 8 per cent nickel and 18 per cent chromium to iron produces austenitic stainless steel, known generically as the AISI 300 series. Austenite is the γ phase of the iron carbon diagram that becomes extensively modified by the addition of 8 per cent nickel, such that the phase exists at room temperature and remains stable down to cryogenic temperatures. Austenite is not attracted to a magnet, unlike ferrite, the normal room temperature α phase of carbon steel and the 400 series of ferritic stainless steels, which are attracted. This property provides a useful means of identification for the austenitic range, although cold working may cause small amounts of retained ferrite to be present, particularly in 304 grades, giving faint levels of attraction to a magnet. It should also be noted that drillings and turnings of austenitic alloys may have been heated and/or cold worked sufficiently during machining to convert some γ phase to α, causing them be attracted to a magnet.

The addition of nickel improves the resistance of these alloys to corrosion in acidic conditions. One of the main features of all of the 300 grades is their ability to be polished to maintain an attractive appearance for long periods of time, thanks to their outstanding resistance to atmospheric corrosion.

One useful property of the austenitic stainless steels, their high rate of work hardening to increase strength, can be a disadvantage in some circumstances. For instance, a bent stanchion or fitting will harden at the bend, making straightening again almost impossible. Similarly, attempts by the owner to make a hole using a blunt drill are doomed to failure, the metal beneath the drill deforming as pressure is increased and becoming increasingly resistant to being cut.

Stainless steels in the 300 series cannot be hardened by heat treatment but products such as sheet, tubes and wire are hardened by cold rolling or drawing. Wire that has been hard-drawn for rigging has a tensile strength that is up to four times that of the cast metal.

Fatigue in metals is a failure mode resulting from the cyclic application of stress. It is often stated that stainless steels are unusually susceptible to fatigue but reference to a wide range of sources shows this not to be the case. In fact the fatigue limits of both 304 and 316 exceed those of most

Principal grades and uses of 300 series stainless steels

Grade	Cr (%)	Ni (%)	C (%)	Others	Properties	Uses
301	17	7	0.10		High strength, high work hardening	Springs, hose clamps
304	18	8	0.06		Multipurpose	Marine equipment, tubing, fasteners, deep drawn items
304L	18	9	0.02		Low carbon minimizes carbide precipitation during welding	Welded parts and other 304 applications
305	17–19	10.5–13	0.12		Low work hardening	Deep drawing, wire
309S	22	12.5	0.05		Oxidation resistant	Heating elements, furnace parts
310S	25	20	0.12		Heat resisting	High-temperature tubes
316	16.5	10.5	0.05	Mo – 2	Pitting corrosion resistance	Marine applications
316L	16.5	10.8	0.02	Mo – 2	Low carbon minimizes carbide precipitation during welding	Welded type 316 applications
321	17.9	0.5	0.02	Ti – 5 × Carbon min.	Titanium stabilized	Heat exchangers to intermediate temperatures
347	18	11	0.08	Mn, Nb + Ta 10 × Carbon	Improved corrosion resistance	Intermittent heating 425–900°C

Mechanical properties of some 300 series stainless steels

Grade	Condition	YS (MPa)	UTS (MPa)	Elongation (%)	Hardness (HV)
301	Cold rolled	927	1235	5	360
	Soft austenitic	230	587	50	150
302	Plain austenitic	250	618	50	170
304		215	505	70	123
310		216	540	40	200
316	Air-cooled 1050°C	278	618	50	180

carbon steels in the soft, normalized condition. The vast majority of fatigue failures that occur in yachting are due to poor design or application of the material, rather than any inherent deficiency of its properties. Chapter 11 covers this failure mode, perhaps the most common in yachting.

Austenitic stainless steels weld very well, although the low-carbon grades 304L and 316L should be used for sections greater than 6mm. Use of the normal higher-carbon versions of these alloys can result in a problem known as 'sensitization', in which chromium carbides are formed in the weld heat-affected zone. This results in reductions in the chromium content of the alloy in a narrow zone on each side of the weld. In service these zones are susceptible to corrosion, known as 'knife-line attack' due to their cut appearance. Low-carbon versions of 304 and 316 reduce the likelihood of the problem, although further protection is provided by the addition of titanium and/or niobium, preferential carbide formers that protect the chromium.

Corrosion problems can also occur if the filler metal has inferior alloy content compared to the parent metal, which can result in galvanic corrosion of the weld. It is common for filler metal to be specified one grade higher (increased levels of alloying elements) than the metal being welded.

The best-quality fittings are made by hot forging, rather than casting, endowing the finished product with a fibrous structure that enhances its strength and fatigue resistance. However, considerable experience is required to produce a forging whose optimum strength matches the applied forces. Perhaps the most famous failures in yachting, the 1992 British Steel Challenge boat forestay failures in the Southern Ocean, were the consequence of poor design/manufacture of the forged fittings, rather than any deficiency of the metal used.

HARDENABLE (400 SERIES) STAINLESS STEELS

Heat-treatable AISI 400 series stainless steels contain iron and chromium plus a few minor elements, particularly carbon. The material has good resistance to atmospheric corrosion and is widely used, perhaps most familiarly to us in stainless steel cutlery and tools. Its use in marine applications has been limited to a few springs and bearings but recently I have come across several cases in which drive shafts have been made from 400 grades, presumably as a cost-saving measure. The alloys have reduced resistance to both general and crevice corrosion when compared with 300 series, which has led to some failures. Furthermore, 400 series alloys are attracted by a magnet, whereas the more reliable 300 series are not. Both ferritic and martensitic grades require heat treatment to develop their mechanical properties.

Properties of ferritic stainless steels

Grade	Type	C (%)	Cr (%)	Ni (%)	Treatment (°C)	YS (MPa)	UTS (MPa)	Elongation (%)	Hardness (HV)
403S17	Ferritic	0.06	13	6	Anneal 700–780	280	416	20	170
	Ferritic	0.06	13	6	Temper 600	510	1158	16	260
430S15	Ferritic	0.1	16.6		Air cool 750	340	540	28	175

Properties of martensitic stainless steels

Grade	Type	C (%)	Cr (%)	Ni (%)	Treatment (°C)	YS (MPa)	UTS (MPa)	Elongation (%)	Hardness (HV)
410S21	Martensitic	0.12	12.5		Oil quench 1000, temper 750	370	570	33	172
	Martensitic	0.12	12.5		Oil quench 1000	1190	1850	2.5	371
420S29	Martensitic	0.16	12.5		Oil quench 960, temper 400	1360	1498	18	480
					Oil quench 960, temper 700	630	757	26	223
420S45	Cutlery	0.32	13		Oil quench 980, temper 180		2780		600
431S29	S80	0.16	16.5	2.5	Oil quench 975, temper 650	695	880	22	270

DUPLEX

A family of stainless steels with chromium content varying from 20 to 28 per cent, nickel 2.5–8 per cent and molybdenum 1–4 per cent is known as Duplex stainless steel. It has exceptional resistance to chloride corrosion and is widely used in difficult seawater service, for example where hypochlorite dosing is used to prevent marine fouling.

Duplex stainless steels have a microstructure that consists of about equal proportions of ferrite and austenite. This combination gives them a number of improved properties, principally increased strength, with yield strengths in the range 400–550MPa, good weldability and toughness. One of the main advantages of these alloys is their resistance to stress-corrosion cracking, a problem to which austenitic stainless steels are particularly susceptible.

The compositions of duplex stainless steels are characterized into groups based on their alloy content and corrosion resistance.

Lean duplex steels contain approximately 21.5 per cent Cr and 1.5 per cent Ni, giving them strength and corrosion resistance superior to that of Type 304L stainless steel. Their higher strength may allow thinner sections to replace components made with thicker sections of stainless alloys like Type 304L.

Standard duplex steel contains around 22 per cent chromium and somewhat higher levels of nickel and molybdenum. The BS970 grade 318S13 is generally known by the name derived from its UNS grade, 2205, and is by far the most widely used version in marine and yachting applications. The alloy exhibits excellent corrosion resistance, much higher than that of grade 316. It resists localized corrosion types like intergranular, crevice and pitting

Mechanical properties of 2205 grade stainless steels

Grade	UTS (MPa)	YS (MPa)	Elongation (%)	Hardness (HB)
2205	621	448	25	293

and is particularly resistant to chloride stress corrosion cracking (SCC).

In production it is annealed between 1020 and 1100°C, followed by rapid cooling. Grade 2205 can be work hardened but cannot be hardened by heat treatment.

Super duplex steels typically contain 25 per cent chromium or more, giving them high pitting resistance, measured by the pitting resistance equivalent number (PREN). Their resistance to all forms of corrosion is very high, making them suitable for use in more difficult industrial applications, including warm seawater.

Duplex stainless steels are increasingly used in yachts today, in duties where conventional austenitic steels have been found wanting. Some examples are skin fittings and ball valves, where the effects of crevice corrosion and pitting can be reduced but not eliminated. Yachts specified for use in tropical waters have been successfully fitted with duplex underwater equipment.

The alloy has been used to substitute for austenitic grades in propeller shafts, increasing their strength while reducing diameter and simultaneously achieving improvements in corrosion resistance.

Grade 2205 is used in the shanks of several stainless steel versions of anchors, where austenitic grades would have insufficient strength to resist bending under lateral loads.

Cromox chain is made from 318LN duplex stainless steel, giving it strength equivalent to Grade 60.

PRECIPITATION HARDENING

Precipitation-hardening stainless steels contain lower levels of chromium and nickel, for example 17 per cent chromium and 4 per cent nickel, plus about 4 per cent copper and other elements. These alloys are heat treated in a complex three-stage process, giving the alloy considerably greater strength than austenitic stainless steel, with equivalent corrosion resistance. Their principal use

Chemical compositions of duplex stainless steels

Grade	EN No/UNS	Type	Approximate composition (%)						
			Cr	Ni	Mo	N	Mn	W	Cu
2101 LDX	1.4162/S32101	Lean	21.5	1.5	0.3	0.22	5		
DX2202	1.4062/S32202	Lean	23	2.5	0.3	0.2	1.5		
RDN 903	1.4482/S32001	Lean	20	1.8	0.2	0.11	4.2		
2304	1.4362/S32304	Lean	23	4.8	0.3	0.10			
2205	1.4462/S31803/ S32205	Standard	22	5.7	3.1	0.17			
2507	1.4410/S32750	Super	25	7	4	0.27			
Zeron 100	1.4501/S32760	Super	25	7	3.2	0.25		0.7	0.7
Ferrinox 255/ Uranus 2507Cu	1.4507/S32520/ S32550	Super	25	6.5	3.5	0.25			1.5

in yachting is in high-performance fittings, such as those made in 17/4PH as Haute Resistance (HR) grade by the French manufacturer Wichard and by Petersen in the UK. For example, the MBL of a 10mm shackle in their HR range is 6000kg, compared with 4300kg in 316L stainless steel.

The expense of the complex manufacturing method is reflected in the price of these fittings.

APPLICATIONS OF STAINLESS STEELS

Stainless steels are used in a wide range of fittings and equipment throughout the modern yacht, from the smallest self-tapping screw, nut and bolt to large winches, windlasses and anchors.

Two grades of stainless steel are principally used for marine purposes: AISI 304 and 316. These two are also known as A2 and A4, respectively, although these designations are more correctly used only for fastener grades. Of these, 304 is the basic 18/8 grade, whereas 316 contains an additional 2 per cent of molybdenum, giving it better resistance to both chloride pitting and crevice corrosion. As a general guideline, 304 should not be used subsea but reserved for on-deck and interior use, although both grades can suffer problems when permanently immersed. Many metals that rely on a passive film for their corrosion resistance suffer from the dual problems of pitting and crevice corrosion, stainless steels being just one example. If a crevice, such as is formed in bolted joints, swaged fittings or nuts and bolts, is immersed in water, the composition of the 'stagnant' water deep inside the crevice differs from the oxygenated water on the outside. This difference causes the metal within the crevice to become active, corroding preferentially due to the fact that the active and passive metals have different galvanic potentials. Pits are themselves small-scale crevices, as is the surface roughness in drawn rigging wire, accounting for the rust stains that can develop on them. Where crevices do not exist, for example on propeller shafts, 316 is widely and successfully used but it is particularly prone to crevice corrosion in wood, where it may be almost permanently wet. This subject will be dealt with more fully in Chapter 10.

Better-quality items for marine use are manufactured by hot drop forging for greater strength and reliability, shackles being one example. Casting is a cheaper method that is perfectly acceptable for low-stress duties such as cleats and fairleads, where the mass of the object provides it with sufficient strength to sustain the anticipated loads. Where items in austenitic grades are required to carry greater stresses than can be sustained by the annealed material, they may be manufactured by cold rolling, stamping or drawing. Examples are wire rope, rigging screws and toggles, tubing and some shackles.

Winch drums are manufactured by a process known as deep drawing. A blank of the metal to be used (in addition to stainless steel, drums of aluminium and brass are made using the same technique) is placed in a forming die and subjected to high force from a tool steel punch. The process is complex and may be carried out in several stages, annealed between each to overcome work hardening.

Bolts and Fasteners
Stainless steel fasteners including bolts, studs, nuts and self-tapping screws are supplied to BS EN ISO 3506. Grades A1, A2 (A3) and A4 (A5) are austenitic grades, C1, C3 and C4 are martensitic and F1 is ferritic.

Chemical compositions of austenitic stainless steel fasteners

Grade	C	Si	Mn	S	P	Cr	Mo	Ni	Cu	Types included
				Chemical composition (max. %)						
A1	0.12	1	6.5	0.15–0.35	0.20	16–19	0.7	5–10	1.75–2.25	303
A2	0.1	1	2	0.03	0.05	15–20		8–19	4	304, 349S17
A3	Composition as A2 with additions of Ti or Nb/Ta as stabilizers									
A4	0.08	1	2	0.03	0.045	16–18.5	2–3	10–15	1	316, 396S17
A5	Composition as A4 with additions of Ti or Nb/Ta as stabilizers									

Mechanical properties of A1, A2 and A4 austenitic stainless steel bolts, screws, studs and nuts

Property class	Diameter range	Bolts, screws and studs (Part 1)			Nuts (Part 2)
		Tensile strength Rm (N/mm^2)	0.2% proof stress (N/mm^2)	Elongation A (mm)	Stress under proof load (N/mm^2)
50	≤M39	500	210	0.6d	500
70	≤M24	700	450	0.4d	700
80	≤M24	800	600	0.3d	800

The high sulphur content of grade A1 makes the steel free machining for ease of manufacture but its corrosion resistance is reduced in marine environments.

Bolts in property class 50 in the annealed condition are usually not marked and are the bolts most commonly supplied by marine chandlers. Bolts in classes 70 and 80 are produced from 'cold drawn' and 'severely cold drawn' bar, respectively. The heads of these bolts are marked with the class numbers and are normally available from specialist suppliers.

Self-tapping screw mechanical properties are defined in part 4 of BS EN ISO 3506. The required values within the property classes are given in minimum Vickers hardness values.

Property classes 20H and 25H apply to either cold-worked austenitic (A2, A3, A4, A5) or ferritic (F1) grades, whereas classes 30H and 40H apply to hardened and tempered martensitic (C1, C3) grades. Marking

Mechanical properties for self-tapping screws (BS EN ISO 3506 part 4)

Property class	20H	25H	30H	40H
Vickers hardness (HV), min.	200	250	300	400

of the grade and property class are shown on the packaging but not necessarily on the screws themselves.

Wire Rope and Cable

Stainless steel rope and cable in one of the 18 per cent chromium, 8 per cent nickel alloys is produced in a number of different grades, dependent upon requirements. Some are less well suited to the marine environment, containing high chloride levels. Type 302 maintains a higher level of ductility than 304 for the same yield and tensile strengths and is the preferred material for some manufacturers. Type 305 work hardens to a lesser extent when deep drawn to the levels required to achieve

Mechanical properties of martensitic and ferritic bolts, screws and studs

Steel group	Steel grade	Property class	UTS (MPa)	YS (MPa)	Elongation (mm)	Hardness HB	Hardness HV
Martensitic	C1	50	500	250	0.2d	147/209	155/220
		70	700	410	0.2d	209/314	220/330
		1103	1100	820	0.2d		350/440
	C3	80	800	640	0.2d	228/323	240/340
	C4	50	500	250	0.2d	147/209	155/220
		70	700	410	0.2d	209/314	220/330
Ferritic	F1	45	450	250	0.2d	128/209	135/220
		60	600	410	0.2d	171/271	180/285

high strength. It is probably the case that most rigging wire in UK and Europe is produced in either 304 or 316, the latter being preferred due to its superior resistance to corrosion in marine atmospheres, thanks to the pitting resistance conferred by its molybdenum content.

Wire rope for yacht applications is produced in three main constructions, 1 × 19, 7 × 7 and 7 × 19. A number of other constructions is made but their use in yachting is unusual.

The 1 × 19 construction stainless steel wire rope is stronger than other types of stainless steel cable and has less stretch. This also means it is non-flexible. It is the construction most widely used for yacht standing rigging where it is not required to bend severely or be used dynamically, for which it is not suited.

The 7 × 7 construction stainless steel wire rope is less strong but more flexible than 1 × 19 strand and yet stronger than 7 × 19 rope. In marine yacht applications it may be used for guard wires and bracing wires requiring some flexibility.

Stainless steel wire rope of 7 × 19 construction is highly flexible. It is less strong

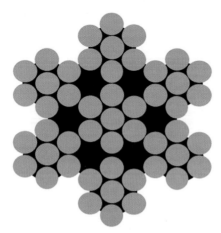

7 × 7 stainless steel wire rope construction.

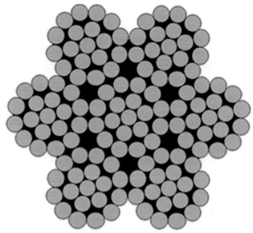

7 × 19 stainless steel wire rope construction.

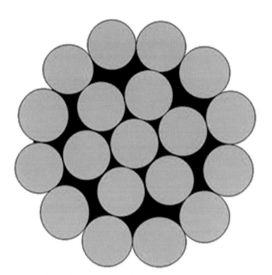

1 × 19 stainless steel wire rope construction.

Dyform stainless steel wire rope construction.

than both 1 × 19 and 7 × 7. It is suitable for most running load applications such as steering systems, halyards and winch cables.

Dyform wire is drawn through a die that provides further deformation, smoothing the outer layers of wire for improved appearance and lower windage but also increasing strength by around 30 per cent and reducing stretch. It is produced in 1 × 19 construction only. This strength increase may allow the user to fit a size

lower than standard, giving further windage reductions.

As with chain, the strength of wire cable is expressed as minimum break load (MBL). A factor of safety of 6:1 is normally applied, that is the safe working load (SWL) is one-sixth of the MBL.

When wire cable that operates dynamically turns around sheaves there is a likelihood of fatigue failure in the individual wire strands. To avoid this problem a universal minimum sheave diameter is

Strengths of 1 × 19 stainless wire rope

Wire diameter	MBL (kg)	SWL (kg)	Weight (kg/100m)
4mm	1350	225	7.9
5mm	2100	350	12.4
6mm	3030	500	17.8
8mm	5040	840	31.7
10mm	7870	1300	49.5
12mm	10600	1766	71.3

Strengths of 7 × 7 stainless wire rope

Wire diameter	MBL (kg)	SWL (kg)	Weight (kg/100m)	Min. sheave diameter (28:1)
4mm	912	152	6.14	11.2cm
5mm	1430	238	9.6	14.0cm
6mm	2050	341	13.8	16.8cm
8mm	3650	608	24.6	22.4cm
10mm	5700	950	38.4	28.0cm
12mm	8270	1378	55.3	33.6cm

Strengths of 7 × 19 stainless wire rope

Wire diameter	MBL (kg)	SWL (kg)	Weight (kg/100m)	Min. sheave diameter (18:1)
4mm	850	141	5.95	7.2cm
5mm	1330	221	9.3	9.0cm
6mm	1920	320	13.4	10.8cm
8mm	3410	568	23.8	14.4cm
10mm	5310	885	37.2	18.0cm
12mm	7660	1276	53.6	21.6cm

Source: Strength data from S3i Group.

quoted for each cable construction type. No minimum sheave diameter is quoted for 1 × 19 cable, which cannot operate in dynamic situations. The values quoted for other constructions relate the minimum sheave diameter to the cable diameter. The preferred minima, above which failure is improbable, are 42:1 for 7 × 7 and 24:1 for 7 × 19. Critical minima are lower than these, as shown in the tables above.

Swaged End Fittings
The ends of wire rope are attached to the mast, deck and other fixtures by special terminals in a wide variety of forms such as eyes, fork ends, rigging screws and others. For wire rope these fittings are made in stainless steel in the soft, annealed condition. Swaging is the action of compressing the fitting metal into the lay of the rope, normally carried out in a manual machine that compresses and extrudes the metal between two dies. The appearance of the swaged end is characteristic, metal being pressed between semi-circular dies with two extruded lines between them. On cutting a swaged fitting open the considerable extrusion of the metal into the lay of the rope is very evident.

Swaged end fitting.

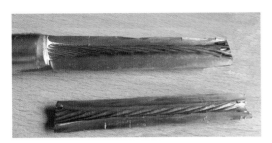

Swage interior.

Galvanized Carbon Steel

Traditional boats continue to use galvanized steel wire that is normally zinc coated to provide protection from marine corrosion. Cables of this construction are strong and may give more warning of failure than does stainless steel. The lower cost is usually a consideration in the selection of galvanized carbon steel.

Solid Rod Rigging

Racing and high performance yachts have used rod rigging for some years, taking advantage of high strength, low windage and low stretch as well as long life due to unmatched corrosion resistance. The material most used today is Nitronic 50, an austenitic stainless steel that has a yield strength about twice that of 316. Its complex composition accounts for its high cost.

End terminals in rod rigging are fitted over the rod, which is expanded to retain the fitting.

Composition of Nitronic 50 (%)

	Min.	Max.
C	0.030	0.050
Mn	4.0	5.5
P		0.040
S		0.015
Si	0.020	0.060
Cr	20.50	22.0
Ni	11.75	13.0
Mo	2.0	2.50
Cu		0.75
N	0.24	0.30
Ti		0.020
Al		0.020
B	0.0008	0.0025
Nb	0.12	0.20
Ta		0.10
Sn		0.030
V	0.10	0.30
W		0.015

CHAPTER 4

Copper and its Alloys

STANDARDS

The standards in general use for copper and its alloys can be very confusing. Although the Europe-wide EN standard applies, it is very common for alloys to be referred to by their old British Standards and USA ASTM designations. I have tried to keep to EN standards throughout this section but conversions to BS standards are included below.

The standards used in this section refer to the EN system, which is very similar to, but may not be identical with, the ISO system.

The system uses a six-character, alpha-numeric series, beginning C for copper-based material; the second letter indicates the product form as follows:

B	Materials in ingot form for re-melting to produce cast products
C	Materials in the form of cast products
F	Filler materials for brazing and welding
M	Master alloys
R	Refined unwrought copper
S	Materials in the form of scrap
W	Materials in the form of wrought products
X	Non-standardized materials

A three-digit number series in the third, fourth and fifth places is used to designate each material and can range from 001 to 999. Numbers are allocated in preferred groups, each series being shown below. The sixth character, a letter, indicates the copper or alloy grouping as follows:

Number series	Letters	Materials
000–099	A or B	Copper
100–199	C or D	Copper alloys, low alloyed (less than 5 per cent alloying elements)
200–299	E or F	Miscellaneous copper alloys (5 per cent or more alloying elements)
300–349	G	Copper-aluminium alloys
350–399	H	Copper-nickel alloys
400–449	J	Copper-nickel-zinc alloys
450–499	K	Copper-tin alloys
500–599	L or M	Copper-zinc alloys, binary
600–699	N or P	Copper-zinc-lead alloys

Converting obsolete BS standards to EN alloys

Old BS alloys	EN alloys	Compositional type	Cu (%)	Zn (%)	Pb (%)	Al (%)	Sn (%)	Mn (%)	Al (%)	Fe (%)	As (%)	Ni (%)	P (%)
C101	CW004A	ETP copper	99.9										
C104	CR008A												
C106	CR024A												
CZ106	CW505L	Cartridge brass	70	30									
CZ108	CW508L	Basis brass	63	37									
CZ112	CW712R	Naval brass	62	balance	0.2–0.6		1.0–1.5						
CZ121 and CZ114	CW721R and CW722R	High-tensile brass/ manganese bronze	58		0.8–1.6		0.2–1.0	0.8–1.8	0.3–1.3	0.2–1.3			
CZ121	CW614N	Free-machining brass	68	39	3.0								
CZ130	CW624N	Leaded brass	56	balance	1.6–3.0	0.5–5.0							
CZ131	CW606N	Riveting-quality brass	62	balance	1.5–2.5					0.2 max.			
CA104	CW307G	Aluminium bronze	balance	0.0–0.4				0.0–1.0	8.5–11.0	4.0– max. 4.0		4.0–6.0	
PB102	CW451K	Phosphor bronze	balance	0.0–0.2	0.0–0.2		4.5–5.5			0.0–0.1		0.0–0.2	0.01–0.4
CZ132	CW602N	Dezincification-resistant brass		36	1.7–2.8		0.2 max.			0.2	0.08–0.15		
CZ121	CW712R		62	balance	0.2–0.6		1.0–1.5			max. 0.15			

For castings, properties are dependent on the casting process used. This is designated according to the following system:

GS	Sand casting
GM	Permanent mould (die) casting
GZ	Centrifugal casting
GC	Continuous casting
GP	Pressure-die casting

For example, the leaded brass widely used for ball valves is coded CW614N–R420 – referring to wrought CuZn39Pb3 copper-zinc-lead alloy to be supplied to a minimum tensile strength of $420N/mm^2$.

CC750S-GS refers to sand-cast CuZn33Pb2 copper-zinc duplex alloy.

COPPER METAL

Unlike many other elemental metals, pure or nearly pure, copper is widely used, primarily for electrical components on account of its conductivity and also its good corrosion resistance (for domestic water supply).

Copper is produced from a mixture of sources, either recycled scrap, often copper wire from which the insulation has been stripped, so called 'cathode copper', and smaller cast ingots.

Only high-quality scrap is used, although some impurities may be present, including typical alloying elements such as zinc, tin and nickel. Cathode copper is produced in huge electroplating cells the size of football fields. The anodes in the cell are large castings from smelting and refining furnaces, immersed in a solution of copper sulphate and sulphuric acid. A direct current is applied, causing 99.95 per cent pure copper to be redeposited onto the negatively charged cathodes. Copper

ingots are made from re-melted cathodes or refined scrap on a smaller scale, usually produced by local recyclers.

The raw materials are loaded into a furnace that may contain 20 tons of metal and heated to a temperature some 200°C above its melting temperature, 1085°C. Oxygen is then introduced into the melt, reacting with impurities to form oxides, which float on the surface and combine with the slag. In a process that is centuries old, green wood poles are plunged into the melt, creating a violent action that assists with the oxidation reaction. Finally, controlled amounts of phosphorus are added to remove the remaining oxides, these also combining in the slag. When this is removed the copper melt is 99.9 per cent pure.

Electrical Uses

Pure copper has the highest electrical conductivity of any commercial metal. This property makes it the preferred material for cables, motor wire, printed circuit board conductors and a host of other electrical applications. Copper has sufficient strength, ductility and hardness for these applications at operating temperatures up to 100°C.

Many different grades of copper are available but for the majority of electrical applications electrolytic tough pitch copper is selected. This term denotes that some oxygen is present, to a level of about 0.04 per cent, possibly with small amounts of silver to 0.002 per cent.

The addition of silver to pure copper improves its mechanical properties with very little effect on electrical conductivity. The amounts are very small and typically in three ranges: 0.03–0.05 per cent, 0.06–0.08 per cent and 0.08–0.12 per cent. This copper alloy is preferred when resistance to softening is required as in commutators or in duties where stresses are applied for extended periods at elevated working temperatures, as in large alternators and motors.

Leadframes (pronounced 'leedframes') are used in almost all semiconductor packages. A leadframe is a thin layer of metal that connects the wiring from tiny electrical terminals on the semiconductor surface to the large-scale circuitry on electrical devices and circuit boards. Leadframes were previously made in aluminium and some are still made from plated ferrous alloys, but the development of more advanced microchips has required the production of copper alloys as leadframe materials with properties to suit the need for long, reliable life at elevated temperatures. The properties required are ductility, strength and springiness, in addition to top-rate electrical and thermal conductivity.

Many copper alloys are produced for this purpose, alloying elements including silver, cobalt, chromium, iron, magnesium, nickel, phosphorus, silicon, tin, titanium, zinc and aluminium.

Tubing

Copper tubing is produced by extrusion, a process that can be likened to squeezing toothpaste from a tube. A billet of the hot copper is pressed through a die by a hydraulically driven ram, producing a large tube up to 25m in length. The tube produced by the extrusion process is about 70mm in diameter and is reduced to the desired size by a process of drawing, which is pulling it through steel dies in several stages. This process is carried out cold, which work hardens the copper. Copper tube is sold in either the hard (or rigid) condition, as it leaves the drawing process, or after annealing at about 700ºC, in half-hard or soft condition.

Hard copper cannot be bent to form curves, needing either soldered elbows or to be annealed during installation. This form of copper tubing is common in continental Europe, whereas soft tubing is more usual in the UK.

Copper tubing is used in a variety of duties in yachts, including for fuel, lubricants, domestic water, heat exchangers and calorifiers. It shows good long-term resistance to all of these gases and liquids, including seawater. Very similar tubing is used for air conditioning and refrigeration applications.

Antifouling

Copper has been used on the hulls of ships for centuries to deter the growth of marine organisms that reduce the performance of the vessel and, in wooden ships, destroy the timbers of which it is constructed. The copper was originally applied in sheet form nailed to the hull, but modern antifouling is mostly applied in the form of paints and suspensions, although there have been attempts to replicate the sheet metal approach. The biocide is in fact copper oxide, which develops a short time after application. Pure

Mechanical properties of BS EN 12449 seamless, round tubes for general purposes

Material	Temper	Tensile strength (N/mm², min.)	Elongation (%, min.)	Hardness (HV)
R220	Annealed/soft	220	40	40–65
R250	Half-hard	250	20	70–100
R290	Hard	290	3	95–120

copper is almost always used, although copper-nickel alloys do have an antifouling effect. Other alloys appear to be ineffective in controlling marine organisms.

It is difficult to prevent marine fouling on propellers. The high flow rate of water over the blades tends to remove paint films quickly, exposing the base alloy beneath, to which slime and shell attaches quite rapidly when the boat is at rest. An additional factor is that paint adhesion to manganese bronze is difficult. A possible solution is to copper plate the propeller. Copper is anodic to manganese bronze and thus there is no risk of corrosion of the propeller itself. The photos show an ongoing experiment to determine whether the technique is worth pursuing. A new manganese bronze propeller was purchased for the test and plated using an acid method. It was mounted on a boat and left on a drying mooring for a period of six months.

After this period the copper had blackened due to the formation of copper oxide but was totally free of fouling, unlike the conventionally antifouled hull that had attracted various organisms.

Manganese bronze propeller.

The propeller was plated with copper.

The same propeller after six months.

COPPER ZINC – BRASSES

Composition of Copper Alloys

The table below shows typical compositions of various copper alloys. Note that these can vary considerably and the table should not be considered definitive. For instance, Admiralty bronze is a 70/30 alloy with additions that may be either 1 per cent tin or 2 per cent aluminium plus a small amount of arsenic. There is even at least one variety of manganese bronze that does not contain manganese!

70/30 Brass

Alloys of copper and zinc form a number of phases, dependent upon proportions. At zinc contents up to just below 40 per cent the alloy comprises a single α phase that is ductile and has good elongation. These are known as the alpha brasses. They can be extensively deformed by rolling, drawing, bending, spinning, deep drawing, cold heading and thread rolling. The most common commercial alloy with this composition is 70/30 brass, used for sheet, rod, tube and wire that may be formed easily. The alloy is sometimes known as cartridge brass thanks to its use for this duty, being deep drawn at room temperature to form the cases of all types of ammunition. Typical uses on boats are for tubes in some heat exchangers, often with the addition of 1 per cent tin, in which case it is known as Admiralty brass, or 2 per cent aluminium for enhanced corrosion resistance. Other uses are the cases of cheaper barometers and clocks (more expensive ones being sand cast in 60/40 brass), hinges and interior lights.

Annealing is typically carried out at 600–650°C.

This brass alloy has good corrosion resistance to weathering and very good

Compositions of brasses in common use (%)

Alloy composition	Cu	Sn	Zn	Pb	P	Al	Fe	Mn	As	Ni	Si
60/40 brass (Muntz metal, Tonval; CW617N)	60		37–40	up to 2.5							
Admiralty bronze	70	1	29								
Manganese bronze	58	1	38			1	1	2			
Naval brass (CW619N)	About 60	1	39–44	1–3							
MS 58 (CW614N)	About 60		39	3							
DZR brass (CW602N)	62	0.7	35.2	2					0.1		

Mechanical properties of 70/30 brass

Condition	YS (MPa)	UTS (MPa)	Elongation (%)	Hardness (HB)
Chill cast	93	247	65	60
Hard rolled sheet	386	463–618	10–15	150–200
Annealed sheet	93	309–355	65–75	60

resistance to many chemicals. It may undergo dezincification in stagnant or slowly moving salt solutions, brackish water or acidic solutions. It suffers stress corrosion cracking in contact with ammonia or ammonia compounds, a property that became a considerable problem during the First World War, when ammunition stored close to stables became liable to exploding in the breeches of guns.

60/40 Brass

As can be seen in the phase diagram, an alloy of 40 per cent Zn, 60 per cent copper is composed of two phases, α + β and has the highest strength of any of the possible range of compositions, but elongation, and therefore ductility, are low. Whereas the 70/30 alloy is quite ductile and can readily be drawn or formed to shape, this is not true of the 60/40 alloys, which are typically cast.

The significance of the dotted line at 453ºC is that the solubility of zinc in α-solid solution increases as the temperature falls to this value, contrary to general behaviour. It then decreases down to room temperature. This property is used in the manufacture of hot-stamped parts in dezincification-resistant (DZR) brass. The line at 470ºC is the temperature above which β phase suddenly softens, making manufacture by extrusion and hot stamping particularly advantageous.

The alloy is frequently known as Muntz metal, after its inventor. The leaded version is known as Tonval, CW617N or CZ122.

Small amounts of lead, in amounts between 1.5 and 3.5 per cent, are often added

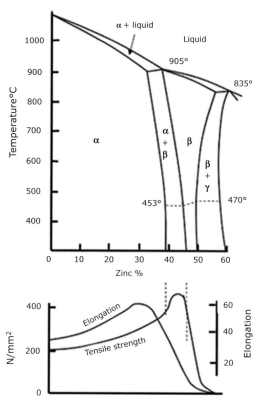

Copper-zinc phase diagram.

to 60/40 brass as an aid to machining properties and for hot stamping and extrusion. Tensile strength is not greatly affected by these additions but elongation may be a little less. Lead is insoluble in both the liquid and solid states and is seen under a microscope as small globules in the brass. Turnings of leaded brass do not form as spirals but break into small pieces.

Mechanical properties of 60/40 brass

	UTS (MPa)	Elongation (%)	Hardness (HB)
Cast	340–386	40–45	90–100
Hard	494	17	131

The biggest use of this alloy on boats is for all types of plumbing fittings, including skin fittings, ball valves, hose tails, compression fittings, elbows and many others. For gas and fuel duties the life of such parts is indefinite but in seawater they are susceptible to dezincification.

Manganese Bronze

Since the nineteenth century many attempts have been made to improve the resistance of brass to seawater corrosion. Small additions of other metals such as tin and manganese have brought about significant improvements, although perhaps not quite as much as their names would suggest – for example neither Admiralty bronzes nor manganese bronze are bronzes at all. The compositions of the 70/30 and 60/40 versions are shown in the table above.

Propellers and P-brackets are frequently made in manganese bronze, the additions of tin and manganese giving a slight improvement in strength and corrosion resistance over 60/40 brass in seawater and mildly acidic conditions.

Another modified version of 60/40 brass, known as naval brass, has somewhat better corrosion resistance than the standard version. The alloy is sometimes sold under the standards MS56 (CuZn44Pb2, CZ130) or MS 58 (CuZn39Pb3, CZ121).

Dezincification

All of these modified brasses have been susceptible to a particular type of corrosion known as dezincification. When immersed in seawater there is a tendency for the zinc-rich phase in brass, and its modified versions, to be leached away, leaving the copper-rich phase behind. Copper has little strength, especially as loss of the zinc leaves it spongy, and the component will fail readily at small loads when this happens. In a well-known case, a boat named the *Random Harvest* sank when a skin fitting failed due to dezincification. However, the answer to the dezincification problem has been known for fifty years and DZR (dezincification-resistant) brasses have been available for almost that length of time.

DZR is a leaded brass with a small arsenic content. Its copper content is very carefully controlled, at about 63 per cent. At copper contents over 63 per cent brass is normally single α phase, so more malleable and used for forgings and so on. Below 63 per cent it is two-phase, mostly used for castings. In the case of DZR the copper level is such that components can be made by hot stamping but converted from duplex to α phase by subsequent heat treatment.

Although yacht owners may believe the alloy to be only necessary in seawater service it is also used in soft waters, where dezincification can be a problem. (I can vouch for this as I have seen the problem at home.) Valves and fittings in DZR are available at plumbing suppliers', no doubt cheaper than in chandleries. They should be marked as DZR.

Most good-quality fittings are now made from DZR, Blakes seacocks being one example, giving them Lloyd's approval for use in a marine environment. If buying underwater fittings and components from a chandlery you should insist that they are DZR, preferably with some form of certification. In 2013 skin fittings and hose tails marked with the CR logo became more

Mechanical properties of manganese bronze CW721R

	UTS (MPa)	YS (MPa)	Elongation (%)	Hardness (HB)
Hot-rolled bar	440–500	180–270	20–12	100–140

widely available from chandleries. Unfortunately it is not possible to differentiate between brass and DZR other than by these markings. My experience has been that only brass valves are chromium plated, whereas DZR valves are left in their natural colour.

Dezincification in used components is fairly easy to see. After abrading away any surface paint and oxidized layers, inspect the bright surface for any sign of pinkness. If this is present you are looking at the copper that remains. The problem affects the surface first, so further abrasion may well remove the entire affected layer. Although mainly seen on underwater components it also occurs on engine water pumps, where the cover is often made from 60/40 brass.

COPPER TIN – BRONZE

Bronze has been known as a moderately strong, corrosion-resistant alloy for thousands of years. The discovery that additions of relatively small amounts of tin to

The nut has been filed flat, removing the remains of its castellations. This shows the cause of the corrosion to be dezincification of the brass. The central parts of the prior castellations retain the yellow colour of brass but exterior regions and the upper surface of the nut between the castellations show the pink colour of copper from which the zinc has been lost.

A nut used to retain a propeller on its shaft. Over a period of around fifteen years the nut, made in 60/40 brass, has lost its castellations due to corrosion.

DZR brass is identified in Europe either by the letters DZR or the logo CR (corrosion resistant). It is now possible to buy skin fittings, ball valves and hose tails in this material.

copper produced an alloy capable of shaping into useful implements had profound influences on the development of mankind, and of course led to the naming of a couple of millennia. Bronze cannon recovered from beneath the sea after hundreds of years are testimony to the excellent corrosion resistance of the alloy, although it has to be said that many of them probably contained more tin than is used today.

The photo below shows a bronze nail extracted recently from the lightship previously stationed at Seven Stones off the Scilly Isles. Built in 1879, she is the oldest surviving wooden light vessel still afloat in the UK and is currently the headquarters of the Royal Northumberland Yacht Club at Blyth. Although the photograph is somewhat blurred it is sufficiently clear to show no deterioration whatsoever after immersion in seawater for a period approaching a century and a half.

In the UK the most widely used bronzes are CT1, LG2 and LG4, where CT stands for copper tin and LG stands for leaded gunmetal in the obsolete BS 1400 designation. It is normally easy to recognize whether a metal is made from bronze or brass by its colour, bronze having a distinct redness compared with brass, hence its American name of 'red brass'.

The addition of tin to molten copper as the casting melt is being prepared causes some tin oxide to be formed. Tin oxide is heavy, insoluble in the molten bronze and remains mixed with it. The resulting castings are weak, porous and may appear

A seawater strainer fitting made in a cast bronze. The compression fitting in its outlet and a 1.5 in hose tail fitting, both in 60/40 brass, are shown for comparison. The pink appearance of the bronze is characteristic, as is the pale green colour of the verdigris.

dirty when machined. Additions of zinc, or better phosphorus, cause reaction with the tin oxides in the melt, which, being lighter, tend to float to the surface of the vessel where they can be removed. Alloys containing levels of phosphorus less than 0.1 per cent are not true phosphor bronzes; above this figure the tensile properties of the final alloy are improved.

CW451K is the most widely used grade of wrought phosphor bronze in the UK. It has good fatigue resistance, is useful for springs and can be cold formed readily.

Almost all yacht fittings were made from bronze until about the 1960s, when cheaper alloys began to become available. These include on-deck fittings such as cleats, fairleads, bow rollers, windlass parts and underwater ones like rudder pintles, skin fittings, seacocks, intake strainers, shaft bearing housings and many others. Older designs of boats and modern replicas, known as 'classic yachts', continue to favour bronze for such fittings. Most of those on sale today are sand cast.

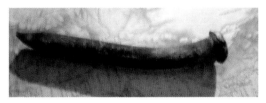

Nail from Seven Stones lightship.

Composition of bronze alloys containing tin

Common name	EN name	Cu (%)	Sn (%)	Zn (%)	Pb (%)	P (%)	Ni (%)
Gunmetal BS-1400 CT-1	None	88	10	0.05–0.5	0.25–1.0		0.1–2.0
BS1400 – LG2	CC491K	85	5	5	5		
BS1400 – LG4	CC492K	88	7	2	3		
Phosphor bronze (wrought)	CW451K, CW450K	93.7	6			0.2	
Phosphor bronze to ASTM B103, B139, B159	None	89	10			0.25	

Mechanical properties of cast bronzes (values dependent upon casting method)

	YS (MPa)	UTS (MPa)	Elongation (%)	HB
LG2	90–110	200–250	6–13	60–65
LG4	130	230–270	12–14	65–70
CT1	130–170	250–280	5–18	60–80

Mechanical properties of wrought phosphor bronze

	Tensile strength (MPa)	0.2% proof stress (MPa)	Elongation (%)
CW451K	460	380	12

The best-quality underwater plumbing fittings are made from bronze, probably LG2 in most cases. Again, they can be differentiated from brass and DZR by their pinker colour. The skin fitting on the right is bronze and that on the left is brass.

Bronzes have been used for decades for yacht components, both above and below seawater. In marine atmospheres a green patina is formed on the surface.

Until around the mid-1980s Blakes sea-cocks were cast in bronze, although they are now made from DZR brass. The bolts provided with them for connection to the hull are made from phosphor bronze for

A very elderly 1.5in elbow made in cast bronze. The mould split line is clearly visible. Its service life is believed to be more than thirty years but it remains in good condition with no visible corrosion. Shown alongside is a new leaded 60/40 brass (Tonval) fitting for comparison. This fitting has been manufactured by hot stamping.

increased strength. Bronze ball valves are available for somewhat more money than DZR ones but the balls within them, either chromium or nickel-plated, have been made in brass, which corrodes away in time. Some stem fittings in bronze valves have also been made in brass, which upon failure by dezincification makes the valve inoperable.

Some rigging or 'bottle' screws continue to be made in bronze, usually chromium-plated, to combat the phenomenon of galling in the more commonly used stainless steel. Galling can cause the threaded parts of rigging screws to become totally welded

together, a problem that is avoided with bronze.

COPPER NICKEL (CUPRONICKEL)

Cupronickel (copper nickel) alloys of copper, nickel and strengthening elements such as iron and manganese exhibit superior corrosion resistance in seawater. The most common alloys are 90/10 and 70/30, both used for marine hardware and piping systems on ships and offshore platforms. A wide variety of piping fittings is available. The high cost of nickel has prevented widespread use of the alloy in production yachts but it may be found in vessels at the top end of the market, superyachts and similar.

Copper nickel alloys with 5, 10 and 30 per cent nickel plus 1–2 per cent iron are available as Cunifer (Kunifer). The 90/10 version is widely used as automotive brake pipes.

Monel 400

I have included Monel 400 in this section although it is more correctly a nickel-copper alloy. Monel 400 is a solid-solution alloy that can be hardened only by cold working. It has high strength and excellent corrosion resistance in a range of acidic and alkaline environments. It also has good ductility and thermal conductivity. Its main use, as far as yachting is

UNS standard compositions of wrought copper nickel alloys

Alloy UNS No.	Common name	European spec.	Ni (%)	Fe (%)	Mn (%)	Cu (%)
C70600	90-10 CN-102	CuNi10Fe	9–11	1–1.8	1	Balance
C71500	70-30 CN-107	CuNi30Fe	29–33	0.4–1.0	1	Balance
C71640	66-30-2-2		29–32	1.7–2.3	1.5–25	Balance
N04400	Monel 400		63 min.	2.5 max.	2.0 max.	28–34

concerned, is as high-cost pop-rivets for masts and spars.

Several other grades exist, including Monel 500, which is used as a corrosion-resistant shaft material for offshore seawater pumps and similar duties. These have not been included in view of their absence from yachting applications.

COPPER ALUMINIUM (ALUMINIUM BRONZES)

Four principal grades of aluminium bronze are produced, each with particular benefits. Other elements routinely added are nickel, iron, manganese, silicon and tin. The mechanical properties of the alloys mainly depend upon the aluminium content, with various benefits provided by the other elements.

Alloys with aluminium content below 8 per cent (aluminium bronze) comprise a single phase and are thus ductile. They are hot or cold rolled to form tube, sheet, wire and strip.

Additions of iron and nickel to alloys containing 8–11 per cent aluminium are strengthened by the formation of a second, β, phase. Alloys in this group have good wear and corrosion resistance. Their duplex structure makes them suitable for hot working and casting. Nickel-aluminium bronze (NIBRAL), with 5 per cent of both nickel and iron, is widely used in propellers

for larger motorboats and superyachts, thanks to its excellent resistance to cavitation and most forms of corrosion.

Aluminium bronzes with around 6 per cent aluminium and 2 per cent silicon are known as aluminium-silicon bronzes. This single-phase alloy is strong and ductile and can be used in wrought and cast forms.

Copper-manganese-aluminium alloys (manganese-aluminium bronzes) are primarily used in the casting of ships' propellers. Manganese to about 13 per cent is added to aluminium at 8–9 per cent plus copper. The resulting alloy has good resistance to cavitation. It is somewhat less strong than other aluminium bronzes but has better casting performance.

COPPER SILICON (SILICON BRONZES)

Two grades of silicon bronze are the most commonly produced – Alloy 651 (ASTM C65100 or CW115C) and Alloy 655 (ASTM C65500 or CW116C).

Silicon bronzes are more corrosion resistant, harder and stronger than brass. Industrially the alloys are used in switchgear, valves and process control equipment. In yachting they are widely used in fastenings such as bolts, screws and nails, particularly in wooden vessels, where it is more corrosion resistant than both brass and stainless

Compositions of various aluminium bronzes (%)

	Cu	Al	Fe	Mn	Ni	Si
Aluminium bronze CC331G	90–93	7–10				
Nickel-aluminium bronze CC333G, CW307G	80	10	5		5	
Aluminium-silicon bronze CW301G	96	6	0.6			2
Manganese aluminium bronze	Balance	8	3	13	3	

Composition of silicon bronze alloys (%)

	Cu	Si	Mn
Alloy 651, CW115C	98	2	
Alloy 655, CW116C	96	3	1

steel, the former suffering from dezincifica-tion and the latter from crevice corrosion when perpetually wet. Boats built using silicon bronze screws and nails are known to survive four and five decades without deterioration of their fastenings. Some modern rigging screws are made in one of the high-strength versions.

Parts in silicon bronze are made by a variety of hot and cold forming methods including drawing, stamping, hot forging and swaging.

Mechanical properties of silicon bronze

	Tensile strength (MPa)	Yield strength (MPa)	Elongation (%)	Hardness (HRB)
CW115C	275	105	50	95
CW116C	745	415	13	213

CHAPTER 5

Aluminium and its Alloys

Aluminium is the third most common element in the earth's crust after oxygen and silicon, comprising 8 per cent. The versatility of aluminium makes it the most widely used metal after steel. Although aluminium compounds have been used for thousands of years, aluminium metal was first produced, very expensively, around 170 years ago. This led to the amusing fact that Queen Victoria owned a full banqueting dinner service made from aluminium.

Aluminium is produced from bauxite, a mineral that is mined in many countries of the world. After purification in the Bayer process the aluminium oxide (alumina) extracted from bauxite is melted in furnace pots that consist of a carbon-lined steel shell. A consumable carbon anode is suspended in liquid cryolite (sodium aluminium fluoride) held within the pot at 950°C. Alumina is dissolved in the cryolite by passing low voltages at high currents through the pot. This results in pure aluminium being deposited at the cathode. Aluminium is tapped off from the pots at regular intervals. Alloying elements are normally added at this stage according to requirements.

In common with most pure metals, unalloyed aluminium is similar to copper in that it is soft, ductile, corrosion-resistant and has a high electrical conductivity. It is widely used for foil and conductor cables, but alloying with other elements is necessary to provide the higher strengths needed for other applications.

The principal properties of aluminium alloys that make them so attractive are a high strength-to-weight ratio and good corrosion resistance. However, the alloying process, particularly the addition of copper, iron and silicon, reduces the corrosion resistance of the alloy. Consequently the 2000, 4000 and 6000 series alloys are commonly anodized to provide a corrosion-resistant finish to articles made from them.

Yacht equipment made from aluminium alloys includes both cast and wrought versions. As with other metals, there are many national and international standards for aluminium alloys, none of which bear any similarity to the others. The most common specification system is perhaps the one provided by the Aluminum Association in USA, applicable to both cast and wrought alloys. In the UK the system provided by BS1490:1988 is commonly used, with designations such as LM2, LM5 and so on.

TEMPER CONDITION

Aluminium alloys are supplied in a very wide range of tempers with two principal groups. Temper is a measure of hardness/strength.

Heat-Treatable Alloys

The strength and mechanical properties of heat-treatable alloys are achieved by heat treatment followed by cooling and natural or artificial ageing. The temper condition is denoted by letter T. The different processes are as follows:

Solution heat treating Aluminium is heated to the prescribed temperature for a prescribed time and then cooled rapidly, usually by quenching in water.

Natural ageing (T1, T2, T3, T4) This process occurs spontaneously at ordinary temperature until the metal reaches a stable condition. This hardens the metal after solution heat treatment.

Artificial ageing (T5, T6, T9) The metal is heated for a prescribed period (2–30 hours) at a prescribed low temperature (100–200°C) until the metal reaches a stable condition. This hardens/increases strength after solution heat treating quicker than natural ageing and to a greater level.

Non-Heat-Treatable Alloys

Non-heat-treatable alloys achieve their strength and mechanical properties by cold working, or work hardening, including rolling, extruding and others. Their temper condition is given by the letter H.

Work hardening (H14) This is a general term for processes that increase the strength of aluminium and reduce the ductility (for example rolling, drawing, pressing, stamping); it is sometimes called strain hardening.

Partial annealing (H24) This is a heating process that reduces strength and increases ductility of aluminium after work hardening; sometimes called temper letdown.

Stabilizing (H34) A low-temperature thermal treatment or heat introduced during manufacture stabilizes the mechanical properties. This process usually improves ductility and is only applied to those alloys that, unless stabilized, gradually age, often at room temperature (that is the non-heat-treatable range). The purpose of stabilizing is to relieve the residual internal stress in the metal. It is mainly used for 5000 series alloys.

CAST ALUMINIUM ALLOYS

Casting has been carried out since prehistoric times. Essentially it involves melting the metal in a furnace, then decanting or pouring it into a hollow mould. Although the mould has traditionally been formed in sand, the modern aluminium casting industry uses a variety of techniques such as metal dies for improved efficiency. Few of these are applicable to the relatively small consumption of the leisure yachting industry but they are shown here for completeness.

Gravity die casting Molten metal is poured into cast-iron moulds. This method produces castings of good surface quality that require little finishing and is used for castings weighing up to about 10kg, sometimes with complex internal cavities. The dimensions are accurate but the finished piece may contain entrapped gases. Aluminium-silicon-copper alloys are mostly used and a typical end product is automotive cylinder heads.

Low-pressure die casting Molten metal is introduced into metal moulds at pressures up to 170KPa. This technique is used to produce automotive wheels and air-cooled motorcycle cylinder heads.

High-pressure die casting This method uses pressures up to 70MPa to force the molten alloy into a massive die. The technique produces a dense, low-porosity

Series	Composition guide	Properties	Applications
1xx	Min. 99% aluminium		Electrical
2xx	Copper	Strong and hard, solution heat treated	Engine pistons, generator housings
3xx	Silicon, copper and/ or magnesium	Sand and die casting	Engine crankcases, tanks, cylinder heads
4xx	Silicon	Good all-round properties; lower corrosion resistance	Widely used for all purposes
5xx	Magnesium	Strength, shock resistance, good corrosion resistance	Marine fittings
7xx	Zinc	Increased strength, less castability	Highly stressed components, airframes
8xx	Tin		Aerospace
9xx	Other		

structure, with excellent wear and fatigue properties, and is used for engine block production. Casting is carried out at 730°C, typically with production runs of 20,000.

Sand casting Moulds are formed by ramming sand onto a pattern. The pattern is then removed, leaving a cavity in the sand.

Shell mould casting The mould is made of a resin-bonded sand 10–20mm thick. Shell mould castings produce finer surface finishes than sand casting and give greater dimensional accuracy.

Plaster casting Plaster slurry is poured around a pattern, the plaster is baked, and the pattern removed, leaving a mould cavity. The operating costs are high.

Investment casting Patterns are made from a wax or thermoplastic pattern that is melted from the mould material, leaving a cavity. This produces accurate castings with good surface finish.

Centrifugal casting The centrifugal casting method forces metal into spinning multiple moulds.

Marine Castings
AA514 (LM5) is probably the most widely used alloy for casting marine hardware such as cleats, fairleads, stanchion bases, mast fittings and similar. All of the 5xx series alloys are non-heat-treatable, with excellent corrosion resistance, machinability and surface appearance, giving them ideal characteristics for these semi-decorative fittings, which are typically supplied in a highly polished condition. Similar alloys are 512, 518 and 535. The castability of the 5xx series is less good than the 3xx series.

The aluminium-silicon alloy A413, equivalent to LM6, is the most widely used aluminium casting alloy. It is ductile and has rather lower corrosion resistance than the 5xx series but it casts well into intricate shapes. It is used for marine castings, as are 384 (LM2) and A380 (LM24), but these two have slightly lower corrosion resistance than A413 and are typically used for interior castings. A380 is often anodized to improve its corrosion resistance and

UK cast grades in the BS1490:1988 designation, with ISO and AA equivalents

UK designation	ISO	AA	Description and usage
LM0	Al 99.5	150	Sand casting. Electrical, chemical and food processing industries
LM2	Al-Si19Cu2Fe	384	Die casting. One of the two most widely used
LM4	Al-Si5Cu3	319	Highly versatile. Heat treatable for increased strength
LM5	Al-Mg5Si1 AlMg6	514	Marine use as sand- and die-cast products. Excellent corrosion resistance
LM6	Al-Si12 Al-Si12Fe	A413	One of two most widely used. Good corrosion resistance and ductility
LM9	Al-Si10Mg	A360	Similar to LM6 but higher strength after heat treatment
LM12	Al-Cu10Si2Mg	222	High strength and shock resistance. Complex foundry methods and heat treatment
LM13	Al-Si12Cu Al-Si12CuFe	336	High thermal stresses, such as engine pistons. Good wear resistance. Requires heat treatment
LM16	Al-Si5Cu1Mg	355	Mechanically strong after heat treatment
LM20	Al-Si12Cu Al-Si12CuFe	A413	Mainly used for pressure die casting. Harder than LM6 with better machinability
LM21	Al-Si6Cu4	308	Similar to LM4 but better machinability and proof strength
LM22	Al-Si5Cu3	319	Used for chill castings requiring good foundry characteristics and good ductility. Requires heat treatment
LM24	Al-Si8Cu3Fe	A380	Large intricate castings where corrosion resistance or ductility is required
LM25	Al-Si7Mg	A356	Good corrosion resistance and thermal properties. Heat treatment needed
LM26	Al-Si9Cu3Mg-	332	Mainly used for pistons as alternative to LM13
LM27	Al-Si 7Cu2Mn0.5		An alternative to LM4 and LM21
LM28	Al-Si 19CuMgNi		Pistons with lower coefficient of thermal expansion than LM13. Special foundry techniques needed
LM29	Al-Si 23CuMgNi		Similar to LM28 but with even lower coefficient of thermal expansion
LM30	Al-Si17Cu4Mg	390	Cast automotive cylinder blocks without liners
LM31	Al-Zn5	712	Good shock resistance. Large sand castings

appearance, although die-cast surfaces are not normally suitable for decorative finishes.

WROUGHT ALUMINIUM ALLOYS

The International Alloy Designation System is the most widely accepted naming scheme for wrought alloys. Each alloy is given a four-digit number, where the first digit indicates the major alloying elements.

The following table is a guide to the compositions of the alloy grades available, although only a limited number are used for marine applications.

Marine Alloys

These alloys are the principal ones used for boat building and shipbuilding, and other marine and saltwater-sensitive shore applications.

Wrought aluminium alloys (AA)

Series	Alloying elements	Applications
1000	Almost pure aluminium (>99%). Good electrical conductivity and chemical resistance	Sheet, foil
2000	Copper alloy, precipitation hardenable to high strength. Brittle and less good corrosion resistance	Aerospace
3000	Manganese alloy, can be work hardened. Good corrosion resistance, especially to pitting	Cans, building, radiators
4000	Silicon alloy	Heat exchangers, engineering
5000	Magnesium alloy. Good resistance to seawater, moderate strength and ductility. Easy to weld	Cans, automobile, building, transportation
6000	Magnesium and silicon alloy. Good resistance to atmospheric corrosion. Easy to extrude and forge	Automobile, building, transportation
7000	Zinc alloy. Highest strength of any aluminium alloy on precipitation hardening	Aircraft industry, radiators

Wrought aluminium alloy compositions (%)

	Al	Fe	Cu	Si	Mn	Mg	Cr	Ti	Zn
1000 series	99.5–99.9						Minor additions of Si and Fe		
2000 series	Balance	0.3–0.7	4–7	<1.2	0.2–1.2	0.2–1.8	Minor Cr, V, Ti		
3000 series	Balance	0.7	<0.25	0.3–0.6	0.4–1.5	<1.3	Minor Zn and Ti		
4000 series	Balance	0.8	0.3	4.5–6.0	0.05	0.05			
5000 series	Balance	0.4–0.7	0.1–0.2	0.25–0.4	0.2–1.0	2.0–5.0	<0.25	<0.25	0.1–0.25
6000 series	Balance	<0.50	0.1–0.4	0.3–0.7	0.1–0.8	0.4–1.4	<0.30	0.10	<0.25
7000 series	Balance	<0.40	0.5–2.4	<0.5	0.1–0.7	0.1–3.7	<0.8	<0.2	4.0–8.0

Marine alloy

	Grade	Applications
4000 series	4043	Filler metal used for 6061 and 6063 welded joints
5000 series	5052-H32 and H34	Cheaper than 5086 but about 20% weaker
	5059-0 and H321	Closely related to 5083. Not heat treatable but can be strengthened by work hardening. Used for boat and yacht hull construction
	5083-0 and H321	5083-0 is the soft grade of this popular boat-building material. Recommended weld filler metal 5183, although 5356 and 5556 may also be used
	5086-H32, H112 and H116	Alloyed with magnesium. Not heat treatable but can be cold worked to increase strength. Excellent weldability that does not affect its mechanical properties. Very successful boat and yacht hull material
	5183	Filler metal used for welding 5052, 5083 and 5086 where maximum strength is required. Also used with 6061 and 6063
6000 series	6061	Precipitation-hardened alloy containing magnesium and silicon. Good weldability, widely used for marine extrusions such as masts, spars, toe-rails. Available as annealed (6061-0), tempered (6061-T6) and stress-relieved (6061-T651)
	6063-T6	Alloyed with magnesium and silicon. Good weldability, heat treatable, good strength. Widely used for extrusions
	6005A	A medium-strength, heat-treatable alloy with excellent corrosion resistance. Its properties lie between those of 6061 and 6082 but its surface finish may be better than either. It is well suited for intricate extrusions
	6082	Lower copper content than 6061, giving it slightly better corrosion properties. Used in high-quality dinghy and yacht spars

Chemical composition of a marine wrought aluminium alloy (%)

Grade	Al	Mn	Fe	Mg	Si	Cu	Ti	Cr
6061	Balance	0.0–0.15	0.0–0.7	0.8–1.2	0.4–0.8	0.15–0.40	0.0–0.15	0.04–0.35

Mechanical properties of a marine wrought aluminium alloy

	Tensile strength (MPa)	Yield strength (MPa)	Hardness (HB)
6061	260 min.	240 min.	95

Aluminium Anodes

Zinc is probably the most widely used anode metal for marine leisure vessels but this metal develops a white layer of zinc hydroxide in fresh and brackish water, preventing its efficient function. In brackish water, or varying fresh/seawater, it is

Typical composition of an aluminium anode alloy (%)

Zinc	3.5–6.5
Indium	0.01–0.03
Manganese	0.01–0.25
Iron	0.2 max.
Silicon	0.10 max.
Copper	0.01 max.
Aluminium	Balance

common to use an aluminium alloy as the anode metal. Aluminium is alloyed with zinc and some minor metals in a variety of ways, a typical composition being shown above.

Aluminium-Hulled Boats

Aluminium is increasingly being used for construction of yachts, in general using all-welded construction in 5086. Not only does this alloy grade provide great strength and resistance to holing, it typically can result in weight savings of 10 per cent over GRP and 37 per cent over timber.

Corrosion is the problem that is most apparent when considering an aluminium boat. Aluminium itself has good resistance to corrosion in both fresh and seawater but it is highly susceptible to galvanic corrosion when in contact with almost every metal in the galvanic series, with the exception of zinc. The oft-repeated story of the copper coin dropped into the bilge of an aluminium boat that subsequently corroded its way right through is probably apocryphal but its roots are undoubtedly based on fact. The two areas that need to be considered very carefully are the connection of fittings made from other materials, mostly stainless steel, and electrical paths.

No metal other than stainless steel should be attached to the hull, with the exception of sacrificial anodes. Fasteners should be plastic or stainless steel, avoiding any copper alloys. Metal objects, such as fishing weights, fish hooks, coins and tools, should not be left in contact with the hull for any appreciable time.

Zinc anodes should be renewed regularly and it may well be worth hanging additional anodes on cables overboard when the boat is berthed, the inboard end attached to the hull.

Electrically, the main requirement is that all wiring is made using twin leads, not using

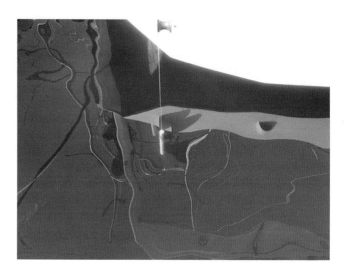

One of four zinc anodes suspended on cables from fixed points, protecting a 42ft aluminium yacht.

the hull for the negative return as is done in automobiles. Shore power should always be checked for polarity. Electrical devices such as isolation transformers and leak detectors are good precautionary measures and should be fitted.

Conventional copper-based antifouling paints would result in galvanic corrosion if applied to aluminium hulls so should never be used. Most paint manufacturers produce copper-free paints specifically for aluminium hulls. Some fouling organisms are known to create conditions that render aluminium more susceptible to corrosion.

Saildrives are increasingly common on the yachts of today and the same rules apply. Copper-based antifouling paints should not be used on them. The recommended paint system should be applied regularly to prevent local attack. Volvo saildrives are isolated from the engine and the remainder of the boat by rubber and plastic insulators and these should not be compromised by additional wiring, or even dirty oil on the gasket. Yanmar saildrives are not isolated in the same way. Both rely heavily on zinc anodes attached ahead of the propeller and these must be replaced in good time.

ANODIZING

Anodizing is the process by which the protective oxide film on the surface of aluminium is artificially thickened. It is thus not a coating but is a conversion of the parent metal. Anodized films protect the metal from corrosion and provide a durable and attractive finish that can be coloured to improve the appearance of the finished product further.

The anodizing process is carried out in an electric cell. The object to be treated forms the anode of the cell, with cathodes attached to the cell walls. The electrolyte in the cell is an acid, typically sulphuric acid. A direct electric current is passed between the anode and cathode, causing oxygen to be formed at the anode, which combines with the aluminium to form aluminium oxide. The oxide film formed is porous and needs to be sealed to harden and solidify the surface. In some cases the sealant incorporates a coloured dye. A variety of methods is used for these final stages.

The thickness of the anodized film depends upon the length of time for which the object is exposed to the anodizing process. Film thickness is specified to cope with the intended application:

- 25 microns for marine and heavy-duty architectural duties
- 15 microns for most general-purpose exterior duties
- 10 microns for interior duties and some decorative exterior duties where frequent cleaning is likely

CHAPTER 6

Zinc

ANODES

Zinc anodes are the most common types used in leisure marine vessels, protecting either single metals or combinations of several, as in the case of propellers, perhaps folding or feathering types, on stainless steel shafts. They are produced in a wide range of configurations, as follows:

- **Hull anodes**, usually with two fixing points as a strap cast into the anode with mounting holes for fasteners; cast in pear-drop or rectangular shape
- **Discs**, usually with a single fastener fixing for steel rudders
- **Shaft anodes**, annular-shaped in two halves that bolt together around a drive shaft
- **Saildrive anodes**, specifically shaped to fit saildrives adjacent to the propeller

- **Engine anodes**, pencil-type anodes that are mounted inside raw-water-cooled engines

In many cases any of these anodes may be supplied with mild steel reinforcing or attachment straps and in the case of hull anodes, with mild steel bolts. The zinc metal protects the steel and there are no corrosion issues except when the boat is ashore and galvanic corrosion no longer applies. In these circumstances there can be corrosion of the steel parts but this is rarely a problem.

Most good-quality anodes are produced to US military specifications.

Although it is possible to recycle old zinc anodes by melting and recasting, great care should be taken to ensure no contamination. Even the smallest traces of iron can inhibit the protection provided. For the same reason it is advised that steel

US military specification for composition zinc anodes (%)

ASTM-B-418 TYPE I MIL-A-18001-K		ASTM-B-418 TYPE II	
Fe	0.005 max.	Fe	0.0014 max.
Pb	0.006 max.	Pb	0.003 max.
Cu	0.005 max.	Cu	0.002 max.
AI	0.1–0.5	AI	0.005 max.
Cd	0.025–0.07	Cd	0.003 max.
Zn	Balance	Zn	Balance

wire brushes and files should not be used to clean anodes before reuse.

Over-Protection

It is possible for anodes to be too large or too numerous, in which case they generate a higher current than is necessary to protect more noble fittings. The result can be hydrogen blistering of antifouling paint or similar coatings on fibreglass hulls. The phenomenon is described as cathode disbondment.

Removal of antifouling systems in itself will lead to an increase in fouling but there is also a tendency for calcium carbonate-based shell and corals to be attracted to the areas surrounding excessive protection. Large accumulations of these white deposits can occur.

The acidity of regions surrounding excessively large anodes can reverse to become alkaline. This is particularly damaging to wooden hulls due to the destruction of essential lignin in the timber, resulting in rot. With metal hulls alkaline conditions will accumulate where water flow is too low to wash away the alkalinity, for example in enclosed areas or during lay-up afloat, and can result in rapid corrosion of the adjacent metal.

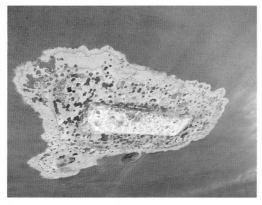

Anode over-protection.

GALVANIZING

Other than anodes, the main use for zinc in boating is as a protective coating for steel to prevent corrosion. Structural items are occasionally galvanized but the most common use is on chain, shackles and anchors that are to be used sub-sea. All of these are likely to be coated in a process known as hot-dip galvanizing, where the steel component is passed through a bath containing molten zinc metal. Zinc may also be applied in an electroplating process, but items coated by this method are unlikely to be ideal for duties where the primary requirement is protection from a marine environment.

The hot-dip galvanizing process follows these steps:

1. The steel is cleaned by passing it through a caustic solution that removes oil and grease. Small amounts of paint may be removed, but where the item has been thoroughly painted it is burnt off or grit blasted.
2. The steel is washed in water to remove the caustic deposits.
3. It is then pickled in an acidic solution, either hydrochloric or sulphuric acid being commonly used, to remove any mill scale.
4. Then it is washed in water again to remove acid deposits.
5. The steel is dipped into a flux solution, typically zinc ammonium chloride, that ensures thorough wetting of the item by the molten zinc.
6. The steel is then dipped into the molten zinc bath and held there until its temperature reaches that of the molten zinc, about 460ºC.
7. Finally it is quenched in water to cool the item and to prevent any reaction between the molten metal and the air.

Unlike a painted finish, galvanizing forms a metallurgical bond between the zinc and the steel, forming a series of intermetallic compounds that roughly comprise Zn/Fe 75/25, 90/10, 94/6 and 100/0 from the steel to the surface. New galvanized surfaces are bright and shiny but within a short time exposure to the atmosphere allows a film of zinc carbonate to form, which provides some additional corrosion protection.

Again, unlike a paint film, the zinc is anodic to the steel and protects it, corroding preferentially when exposed to water, even when small amounts of damage have caused areas of the steel to be exposed.

Anchors are galvanized in a batch process, using baskets that contain a number of them. The baskets are shaken to remove excess zinc before the final quench operation. Chain may also be galvanized in a batch process but in this case there is a risk that links will be 'welded' together when cooled. Alternatively chain can be galvanized using a continuous process that avoids this problem but is rather more expensive.

After a life that may vary between three and fifteen years the zinc will all have been consumed, at which stage it can be restored in a regalvanizing process, following the same steps. Paint may need to be removed by burning off, which is accomplished by immersing the item in the molten zinc bath without passing through any of the preceding processes.

Galvanized surfaces that remain wet for long periods will develop a white surface film that is mostly zinc hydroxide. Because this film is consuming the zinc metal that provides corrosion protection it is preferable to keep items such as anchors and chain dry whenever possible, particularly during the winter lay-up ashore. Hanging the chain beneath the boat keeps it out of the worst of the weather and allows air to circulate through it to dry it when it does get wet.

Unfortunately not all zinc-coated marine components are hot-dip galvanized. Several other methods are available, including electroplating, which gives a bright appearance but offers less protection from corrosion. Items treated in this way are known

Chain regalvanized in a batch process. The wires used to lift the bundle of chain into each stage of the process remain attached.

Chain hanging from bow cleats, suspended on a length of timber. Air circulates through it, drying rain as quickly as possible.

A nice example of the way zinc corrodes when kept semi-permanently wet. My chain was suspended on a rope tied between two legs of the cradle on which the boat sat. The rope remained wet for extended periods when it was tied to the galvanized legs of the cradle. The zinc has corroded at this precise point, forming zinc hydroxide 'white rust'.

as bright zinc plated (BZP). One example is the C-link, used to connect lengths of chain together while allowing the total length to pass through a windlass. Most types corrode quite rapidly by comparison with the chain they are connecting. Two examples

are shown – one connecting galvanized to stainless steel chain, the other connecting two galvanized lengths. In each case the C-link is badly corroded, suggesting that a possible galvanic reaction does not apply.

BZP C-link connecting stainless steel to galvanized steel chain.

BZP C-links in a galvanized chain.

CHAPTER 7

Lead

Lead is not widely used in boat construction, but when it is its principal useful property is its weight. The specific gravity of lead is 11.3, which means it is about 1.5 times heavier than iron and steel at 7.8, or brass at 8.5. Where high weight and low volume is important, such as in the keels of performance yachts, lead is the metal of choice.

KEELS

Lead keels are typically cast in sand that is packed around a wooden pattern of the final shape. The sand is broken away and reused after each cast, whereas for longer production runs a ceramic-based lead keel mould can be made and can be used fifty or more times. It is normal for keel bolts to be cast into the keel, the bolts often being bent into a J shape to add strength.

In most cases the bolts in an iron keel are drilled and tapped after casting but the poor mechanical strength of lead is insufficient to prevent bolts attached to lead in this way from pulling through the metal. In most modern keels the bolt material is 316 grade stainless steel, although bronze has been widely used in the past.

In traditional wooden boat construction of long-keeled designs it was normal for keel bolts to be drilled right through the timber keelson and the casting, with the bolt heads let into the bottom of the lead. The bolts in the eighty-year-old boat shown below are made from bronze that remains in sound condition, and are believed to be original. The countersunk head of the bolt is at the lower, exterior side of the keel with nuts on the inside of the boat.

Modern high-performance racing yachts have composite keels that are fabricated from steel in the narrow upper parts attached to the hull and a lead torpedo at the bottom. The ballast is thus placed as low as possible to increase righting moment while minimizing drag through the water.

BATTERIES

Although various other metals are used to provide electrical power and storage in boats, lead batteries remain the most common type. A battery cell consists of a positive plate made from lead metal coated with a paste of lead dioxide and a negative plate made from porous lead. An insulating separator is located between them. The plates are submerged in an electrolyte of dilute sulphuric acid. A cell in good condition produces 2.1 volts that is combined in series with other cells in a battery producing 6.3, 12.6 or 25.2 volts.

Bronze bolt in lead keel.
JONATHAN
RYDER-RICHARDSON

Plates are made as grids, into which the lead dioxide paste can be pressed. Because grids made of pure lead would have insufficient strength to support their weight, alloying elements are added to improve mechanical properties; 8–12 per cent antimony has been used since 1881 and calcium since the 1930s. Each have disadvantages, antimony improving deep-cycling at the cost of increased outgassing of hydrogen, which means more frequent topping up of water, whereas calcium reduces levels of self-discharge but is less tolerant of overcharging. These are sometimes described as lead-antimony or lead-calcium batteries. In recent years some other metals, such as tin, arsenic and selenium have all been employed to produce lead alloys that reduce the antimony and calcium content.

A typical sealed lead-acid battery provides 200–300 discharge/charge cycles. After this the positive electrode grid begins to corrode, releasing lead dioxide, which falls to the bottom of the cell and ultimately shorts it out. No action can be taken to arrest or reverse this progress.

Some leisure batteries are made with additional space below the plates to accommodate the material that falls from the plates without causing them to short out.

The plates of starter batteries are about 1mm thick, while the typical leisure or deep-cycle battery will have plates that are between 1.8 and 2.8mm thick. The thin plates of the starter battery provide high currents of short duration while the thicker plates of the deep-cycle type allow lower currents to be drawn for longer periods without plate distortion. Batteries used to supply high currents for long periods, such as in forklift trucks and electric milk carts, may have plates up to 6mm thick.

More recent types of battery include the gel and AGM batteries. In these the electrolyte is not present as a solution but is instead gelified using fumed silica (gel type) or absorbed into a glass fibre mat (absorbed glass mat, or AGM). Their chief advantage is that they can be used in position and do not need to remain upright. Both types have lead-calcium plates that reduce outgassing but are less tolerant of overcharging.

ANCHORS

Some anchors are weighted at the tip by lead that is cast into the triangular volume at the forward end of the flukes. It is essential that this be removed before regalvanizing takes place, as an explosion can result when the lead meets the molten zinc at a temperature some 130°C above its melting point. The galvanizer should be informed if the anchor contains lead, which is usually obvious, as the port through which the lead is added can be seen. If there is any doubt a survey by magnet will reveal the port.

Lead cast into the anchor tip.

CHAPTER 8

Fracture

Engineering metal alloys are almost invariably ductile. This protects them from fracture in the event of accidental overload, upon which they can deform slightly to accommodate the higher stress. The opposite of ductile is brittle, a condition that should never be encountered in the materials used in the boat, with the possible exception of glass. The most common metals in boats, for example aluminium, the various copper alloys and stainless steels, are ductile at all temperatures down to the lowest that can be experienced, but carbon steels display a phenomenon known as the ductile-brittle transition temperature. This is unlikely ever to be a problem for any other than arctic sailors.

The difference between ductile and brittle is characterized by the appearance of the fracture face. Brittle fractures occur in the straight-line or elastic portion of the load-elongation curve, which means that the fractured part returns to its original shape. Brittle fractures therefore display no deformation. In contrast, ductile fractures show high levels of deformation, giving an appearance known as 'necking', due to the reduction in area that occurs in the fractured region.

Whereas ductile fractures take place only due to excessive loading over and above the yield point of the metal, brittle fractures can occur at quite low loads and are therefore unwelcome in any engineering situation. Examination of fracture faces with a microscope or magnifying glass reveals the fundamental difference between the two. In a ductile fracture the crack path tends to be through the grains, or trans-granular, resulting in a rough, dull appearance that is sometimes referred to as 'woody' due to its appearance being similar to a snapped green twig. Brittle fracture paths are inter-granular, giving them a crystalline appearance due to light reflecting back from the crystal faces.

DUCTILE-BRITTLE TRANSITION

Many common materials display a ductile-brittle transition that occurs at a particular temperature. A good example is chocolate. After a short period in a refrigerator a bar of chocolate will snap in a brittle manner without deformation, but after resting for a time in a warm room it becomes ductile and attempts to break it result in deformation and some extension. Mild steels with a carbon content of around 0.20 per cent undergo a transition at around 0ºC but additions of manganese at a ratio of 4:1 manganese:carbon avoids the problem. Engineering steels used for ships' hulls, anchors and chain will usually comply with this composition, avoiding the risk of unexpected fracture.

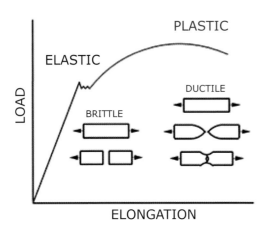

Ductile and brittle fractures.
SID RADCLIFFE

Fractured CQR anchor. ROGER WINTER

BRITTLE FRACTURES

Grey cast iron is also relatively brittle but in general it is made in such large sections, for instance in keels, that the problem does not occur. Engine crankcases are also cast in grey iron, with the result that impacts can cause fractures.

The photo below shows such a fracture, caused when the big-end bearing bolts failed.

CQR anchors are known for being made from forged steel, giving them good strength and the ability to resist heavy force. It is not generally known that those marked up in half pounds, for example 24½lb, are made in cast iron, and there-fore brittle. The photo above shows one that fractured in a brittle mode when 'a navigation buoy jumped out and collided with the anchor'. The two bright areas on each side of the central pin are typical of such failures.

Dezincification is a condition in which the zinc in brass is corroded away, leaving

Crankcase brittle fracture.

CW617N valve brittle fracture.

weak and brittle copper. This is fully covered in Chapter 10 but the photo opposite below illustrates the resulting brittleness of the brass in a ball valve that was leaned upon by the owner of the boat.

The only other circumstances in which brittle fractures can occur in typical marine alloys are where corrosion penetrates between the grains of the metal. The resulting crystalline appearance is characteristic of brittle fracture and is known as inter-granular attack. Several examples are shown in Chapter 10 as stress-corrosion cracking.

FATIGUE FRACTURES

Fatigue is covered in its own chapter (Chapter 11), being a particularly important failure mechanism in yachts. As will be seen, fatigue fractures commence as a crack that propagates through the metal until what remains is unable to sustain the load. The final fracture is almost always ductile in nature but in a few exceptions – due to the crystal structure of the metal – it can be brittle. One such example is nickel aluminium bronze, as used in propeller manufacture.

CHAPTER 9

Joining Metals

Metals are joined by a variety of methods, either permanently, semi-permanently or non-permanently. The principal permanent methods of joining metals are welding, brazing and soldering, all of which rely on the melting of a metal to form the joint, along with the use of adhesives. Non-permanent joining methods are riveting, bolting and other forms of fasteners.

WELDING

Welding is normally carried out between metals of similar composition and is used for carbon steels, stainless steels and aluminium alloys. The parts to be welded are heated to above their melting temperature, forming a puddle of molten metal at the heat source, in some cases augmenting the puddle with filler rod. Methods commonly used may be gas welding, electric arc welding (SMAW), metal inert gas (MIG) and tungsten inert gas (TIG). Some specialist techniques such as friction welding, electron beam, laser welding and others are probably too specialized for the majority of yacht production.

Stick welding, or shielded metal arc welding (SMAW), as it should be known, remains the most widely used form throughout the world. It is perhaps the most commonly used technique for amateur boat building in steel, although with the introduction of low-cost MIG equipment this situation may be changing.

SMAW is most often used to weld carbon steel, of both high and low alloy content, although it is possible to use the technique for many other metals such as stainless steel and some non-ferrous metals such as nickel and copper and their alloys. The minimum thickness that can be welded is about 1.5mm (0.06in) and there is no limit to the maximum due to the use of multi-pass welds. The equipment used comprises a constant current welding power supply and two welding cables, one to an earth clamp and the other to the electrode in its holder. The electrode is a wire of the appropriate metal coated in a flux that protects the molten metal from oxidation and contamination.

In MIG welding the filler rod comes in the form of a coil of wire that is fed automatically into the molten puddle. The arc is shielded from oxidation by the flow of an inert gas, either carbon dioxide or argon or a mixture of these and some other gases. MIG is used for welding a wide variety of metals, including carbon steel, stainless steel and aluminium alloys.

TIG welding uses the heat generated by an arc between a tungsten electrode and the work piece, with filler rod added as necessary in a manner rather similar to gas welding. TIG welding is perhaps the most difficult skill to master but in the right hands produces welds of remarkable quality. The photographs below show the bore and exterior of a length of stainless steel pipe, 4in in diameter with a wall thickness of 1mm.

The composition of the wire is usually similar to that of the steel being welded, but for carbon steel it has been found better for corrosion reasons for the wire to contain small amounts of alloying metal such as chromium and nickel. By making the weld slightly more noble than the base metal the problem of preferential weld corrosion in seawater can be avoided.

Austenitic stainless steels generally weld well, particularly using MIG, but they can suffer a problem known as weld decay, in which a narrow band of the plate, 1–2mm from the weld, corrodes preferentially. The cause of the problem is that chromium-rich carbides precipitate at the boundaries of grains immediately adjacent to the weld, denuding the narrow area of chromium, which is thus vulnerable to severe corro-

TIG welded pipe, bore.

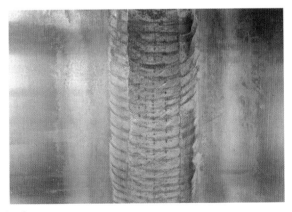

TIG welded pipe, exterior.

sion. Reducing the carbon content of the steel, as in 304L and 316L, can overcome the problem, but for additional effectiveness filler metal with added titanium and niobium, which are strong carbide formers, is preferred. These filler rods are the stabilized versions 347 and 321.

It is common for 304L to be welded using the 20/10 alloy 308L as a filler, whereas 316L is often welded using 316L as the filler.

Home Construction of an Anchor

It is perfectly possible to construct a modern anchor at home, given engineering skills and some fabrication equipment. This impressive anchor has been designed and built by Nuno Santiago, who has kindly provided the detailed photographs and construction information.

This one, the third or fourth constructed by Nuno, was made from 12mm cut plate mild steel and has a ballasted tip in laminated steel instead of lead. This will allow it to be hot-dip galvanized. Special care was taken to eliminate any avoid voids between the plates, and all were deeply chamfered to enable deep weld penetration. The main plates were SMAW welded, but MIG was used for everything else including the shank. All the 12mm plates were edge prepared, and welding was carried out at about 150/160 amps.

1. First steps in the construction. 12mm plate cut to shape, edges prepared by grinding to a chamfer for through-penetration welding.

2. Reverse view of the same parts. The back part of the fluke has a small bend applied to give the final concavity.

3. The three parts are tack-welded together using SMAW (stick welding).

4. Another view of the same, showing the bend of between 15 and 20 degrees.

5. MIG welding commenced, showing the weld preparation forming a V-shape that allows the plate to be joined throughout its thickness.

6. Rear view of the fluke as welding continues. Welding alternately on front and back reduces thermal distortion.

7. The design uses a skeg at the tip to increase loading at this point, crucial to modern thinking on anchor design.

8. The skeg is initially tack-welded using SMAW, then fully welded using MIG.

9. Several further small pieces of plate are added at the back end of the fluke, giving the characteristic concave profile and rounded rear shape.

10. View from the underside before welding is complete.

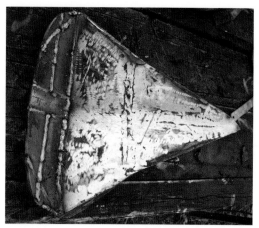

11. Fluke fully welded, top side.

12. Underneath view of the completed fluke, showing the 'wings' at each rear end and the skeg built up of three or four pieces of plate.

13. The shank cut from a single piece of plate, ready for welding to the fluke.

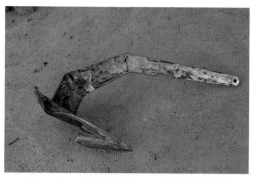

14. Side view of the shank and fluke after welding. The full profile of the design can now be appreciated.

15. End view from the rear of the fluke, showing the concave shape and the curve of the wings.

16. Two narrow strengthening pieces have been added to the shank to enable it to resist bending when lateral loads are applied. This simple design technique adds great strength and avoids the use of high-tensile materials.

17. The finished anchor.

18. When dropped the anchor sets with the tip against the ground and when pulled lays itself down putting a lot of pressure on the (curved) tip, giving confidence that it will work well in practice.

BRAZING

Brazing is mainly used for copper alloys, utilizing a variety of copper-based alloys as the filler rods. The composition of the brazing rod is invariably different from that of the metals being joined, making galvanic corrosion on immersion almost inevitable. Brazing is thus largely confined to joints inside the boat and is particularly used in refrigeration and air conditioning pipework.

In brazing the parent metal is not melted; instead, a gas torch or a TIG welder is used to melt filler rod that has a slightly lower melting point than the work. The molten filler is drawn into the gap between the work pieces by capillary action. The fit of individual pieces of metal before brazing therefore needs to be good to avoid holes in the final work. It is thus similar to soldering except that the filler metal has a higher melting point. The joint produced is strong, the filler metal often being stronger than the work pieces, which can either be the same or of different composition.

In most brazing operations a flux of borax is used to prevent the formation of oxides while the work is being heated. Borax may be used in powder, paste or liquid form. Borax is corrosive when in contact with water and should be removed from joints before going into service.

The most common alloys used for brazing contain three or more metals, selected to melt at the appropriate temperature. Some examples are aluminium silicon for brazing aluminium, many alloys of copper with zinc, silver, tin and phosphorus for general brazing of steel, copper and copper alloys. In addition there are many exotic mixtures of metals that may be used for high-tech applications in aerospace, electronics and others.

TIG brazing does not require the use of a flux thanks to its inert gas shield. The composition of filler rods used in this technique differs somewhat from that used in gas brazing; for example, copper silicon manganese may be used for steel to steel, and copper tin for dissimilar metals such as copper and stainless steel.

SOLDERING

Soldering is the joining of metals, usually but not exclusively copper and its alloys, with low-melting alloys of lead, tin and some others. Again, there is a likelihood of galvanic corrosion if soldered joints are used in seawater but for fresh water, such as domestic supplies, the method is widely used. Most electrical component connections are made by soft soldering although crimped connections in wiring are preferred for their increased resistance to fatigue and higher temperatures with ageing.

Plumber's solder consists of about two parts of lead to one part of tin, solidifying over a range of 240°C down to 183°C, being pasty at the temperature between the two, enabling wiped joints. The addition of 1–3 per cent antimony makes a product known as tinman's solder, which solidifies over a very small temperature range at 183°C. For higher solidification temperatures, tin with 5 per cent antimony or lead with 1.5 per cent silver are used.

Fluxes for soft soldering are either zinc chloride (killed spirits) or resins, both types dissolving oxide films on the surfaces of the metals being joined.

BOLTING

Problems can arise when different metals are joined together by bolting, due to the possibility of various types of corrosion, particularly galvanic corrosion. Perhaps the most common combination is stainless steel fittings attached to various aluminium alloys, on masts, toe-rails, windlasses, steering pedestals and many others. In some cases fittings made from various brasses and bronze may be attached similarly. The combination of metals in dry conditions is not a problem, but wherever seawater splashes or even a salt-laden atmosphere can bridge the different metals there may be a consequence.

In any location where seawater is likely to be present, that is anywhere on the exterior of the boat, it is most common to use A4, 316 stainless steels for bolts, sometimes with A2, 304 for nuts where they are inside the boat to take advantage of their slightly lower cost. Over time A4 is likely to be more reliable due to its increased resistance to pitting.

Brass will inevitably suffer dezincification on board, even inside the boat. Brass screws in interior wood trim regularly snap when being withdrawn after a few years. Bronze bolts have traditionally been used to attach bronze fittings but the material has relatively low strength. Phosphor bronze is used as an alternative, being considerably stronger, but it is very expensive.

Where appropriate, it is worthwhile separating bolted parts using plastic sleeves and washers. In some production small boats stainless steel fittings on flanges are bedded on aluminium structural components using sticky-back plastic as a low-cost, easy method of separating the two metals. This cheap and cheerful technique has overcome a serious galvanic corrosion problem.

The primary precaution in any exterior bolting situation is to exclude water as far as possible by using sealants. Corrosion cannot occur if water is not present. There are many excellent modern sealants on the market, for example polyurethanes and hybrid polymers that have revolutionized boat building and many other fields of engineering. Fittings bedded on such sealants, with their fastenings liberally coated with the same materials, will last almost indefinitely in seawater. My own seacocks are attached with through-hull countersunk stainless steel bolts, well bedded in sealant, that have been performing perfectly for thirty years with no deterioration.

RIVETING

Welding thin metal sheet is increasingly possible using MIG and TIG techniques, although distortion increases as section decreases. Steel and stainless steel sheet down to 1mm can be welded successfully by a skilled operator, but aluminium of less than 3–6mm poses particular problems. These are overcome by riveting, although a different set of problems then arises.

The precautions to be taken in riveting are largely similar to those for bolting, except that in many cases there is a wider variety of rivet materials that can be chosen – aluminium, stainless steel and Monel being possibilities in order of strength. The majority of aluminium masts and spars are constructed using aluminium rivets to attach sleeves and fittings,

thus avoiding the possibility of serious galvanic corrosion. Where higher strength is required to enable fittings to carry bigger loads it may be necessary to use stainless steel rivets. The metalwork hardens significantly during the placing process, which gives them great strength but can require considerable force on the tool to execute. Medium- to long-term galvanic corrosion can be a problem with this combination, which can be alleviated by the use of zinc or barium chromate paste.

The copper nickel alloy known as Monel is almost totally corrosion resistant, occupying the same position in the galvanic series in seawater as passive 300 series stainless steels. It is not susceptible to crevice corrosion and is very strong, making it a useful alternative to stainless steel rivets in some circumstances. Unfortunately it is a very expensive choice and its use should be reserved for special cases.

Since the 1920s it has been known that zinc chromate is beneficial in preventing the corrosion of aluminium and its alloys. In the form of a yellow paste it has been widely used in riveted aircraft manufacture since well before the Second World War, but its use is now extended to many combinations of metals where galvanic corrosion is a possibility. More recently it has been found that barium chromate performs somewhat better than the zinc equivalent and in consequence the product known universally as Duralac is produced as a paste combining a synthetic elastic resin and barium chromate.

All riveted joints on yachts will benefit from the application of a chromate paste, particularly where dissimilar metals are in contact and especially in a marine environment. Similarly, fittings attached by bolts or self-tapping screws are subject to the same galvanic possibilities and will be protected by the use of these pastes.

An alternative approach is provided by a product marketed as Tef-Gel, which comprises a PTFE powder carried in a solvent base. The solvent remains in place without evaporating and thus no voids are created that might draw corrosive waters into a joint. The product works by excluding water from riveted and bolted joints and does not in itself inhibit corrosion chemically.

CHAPTER 10

Corrosion

There are ten recognized types of corrosion, although not all of them are applicable to boats. Below is a summary of the types with brief notes.

General corrosion: The type we are perhaps most familiar with – rusting of unpainted steel being perhaps the best known. The metal does not form a protective film and is liable to attack by water and many solutions.

Galvanic corrosion: When two different metals connected together are immersed in a conducting aqueous solution the metal that is more anodic, that is higher in the galvanic series, will corrode preferentially.

Pitting corrosion: Certain metals that form a protective oxide film, for example aluminium and stainless steels, suffer localized attack where the corrosion is concentrated in specific areas where the film breaks down.

Crevice corrosion: In narrow openings, bolted joints and close fits, particularly in oxygenated aqueous systems, the limited supply of oxygen within the crevice makes it anodic to the surroundings. A concentration cell is established, leading to local metal loss.

Selective corrosion: This is when specific elements from an alloy are removed by corrosion, for example dezincification, denickelification, graphitization. This can also occur where grain boundaries become anodic relative to the grain itself, for example sensitization in welded stainless steel.

Condensate corrosion: This occurs in engines where acidic combustion products are deposited on valves, injectors and liners at temperatures below the dew point. As this is rarely a problem in small boat engines it is not considered further here.

Microbial corrosion: Sulphate-reducing bacteria and theobacilli combine together to cause pitting corrosion in steel fuel tanks. Again, this is rarely a problem in small boats and is not considered further.

Erosion corrosion: Flowing aqueous solutions remove protective films, exposing nascent surfaces that can corrode rapidly. Again, this is rarely a problem in small boats and is not considered further.

Stress corrosion: The combination of stress and corrosive environments accelerates fatigue where the stress is cyclic and can cause severe cracking where the stress is static. Fatigue generally evidences as a single crack, whereas stress corrosion is normally seen as multiple, branched cracking.

Hydrogen damage: This is a form of stress corrosion where tensile stress is applied to a metal that has hydrogen dissolved within it, and is particularly problematic in welded components and hardened steels. The most vulnerable are high-strength steels, titanium alloys and aluminium alloys.

GENERAL CORROSION

Every boat owner knows that iron and steel corrode rapidly in a marine environment, whether it be engines and drive trains and their components, tools, chain, keels or the relatively rare construction parts incorporated into the hull. Coating by zinc galvanizing, paint, oil, grease and resin coating are just some of the ways in which steel can be protected from rusting.

Many drive train parts, such as shaft couplings, are unpainted on purchase and it is well worth rectifying this to preserve them. It is not easy to fully paint Aquadrives, which also are delivered unprotected, and it is easier to keep them greased, or to use Waxoyl, which is useful and long lasting, for the protection of many steel components. Because these parts are sited in the bilge, where seawater is often encountered, they can rust severely in a relatively short time. Here the Aquadrive thrust plate has also been made in carbon steel, with similar results when exposed to seawater.

Some boats are built with steel parts incorporated in their construction, such as frames for the distribution of rigging or rudder loads. These are often galvanized

Corrosion of carbon steel in seawater.
JACK UNDERHILL

or epoxy coated for corrosion protection but regular inspection is necessary. On a Jeanneau Sun Odyssey 45 the rudder is supported by a galvanized steel framework. Water that leaked through the deck seal down the rudder post corroded the top of

Corroded bearing housing. TONY CROSS

Rebuilt bearing structure in stainless steel.
TONY CROSS

the framework containing the upper bearing but was not visible from below without some effort. The frame was rebuilt locally in Greece using stainless steel, redesigning slightly to avoid the possibility of water lying on the structure.

GALVANIC CORROSION

When two different metals are connected together and immersed in seawater, one of them will corrode preferentially. This can be damaging in situations where the corroding metal is perhaps a fastening or other crucial part but it can be used to advantage, for example with anodes.

The rate at which metals corrode in seawater is given by the galvanic series in seawater table overleaf, in which the corrosion rate is given as a voltage by comparison with a standard electrode. The most active metals at the right-hand side of the table – zinc, aluminium, magnesium – are described as 'anodic', and have a negative voltage that is relatively high. Metals at the other end of the scale are 'noble' or 'cathodic', have a voltage close to zero and are thus little affected by seawater. The largest voltages are created by pairing a noble metal with an anodic one, with the result that the anodic metal will corrode quickly. Zinc is the most widely used anodic metal in yachting applications in seawater, both for galvanizing and as sacrificial protection for a range of other more noble metals. In fresh water zinc forms a white oxide or hydroxide that inhibits its action, and thus it is usual to substitute magnesium for wholly fresh-water-based boats. Where the water is brackish, or for boats that regularly voyage from a fresh-water berth onto the sea, it is common to use aluminium anodes.

Where two metals connected together might react galvanically when immersed, for example a manganese bronze propeller on a stainless steel propeller shaft, a third anodic metal connected in addition will protect both by corroding preferentially. It is normal to connect a shaft anode in this case. Some folding or feathering propellers comprise more than one metal, for example bronze hub and blades with stainless steel hinge pins, and in these cases a propeller anode may be needed. Where a shaft anode is inappropriate it is normal to use a hull anode that is mounted close to the propeller and shaft, electrical connection usually being made via the shaft, coupling, gearbox and engine, and thence to the anode by wire. In this case it must be ensured that the coupling itself can pass current.

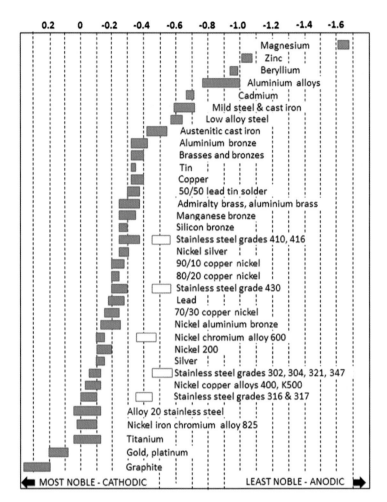

Galvanic series in seawater.

It is a common misconception that an external hull anode is protecting the engine from corrosion, but this is not the case. Electrons in open water travel almost wholly in straight lines, hence the standard advice from anode manufacturers that anodes should be able to 'see' the object they are protecting. Although it is known that electrons will travel along seawater constrained in a pipe it is not the case that a length of hose between a seacock and the engine will act as if it was a wire conductor. Raw-water engines are normally equipped with internal anodes that help to combat internal corrosion, both general and galvanic. Indirectly cooled engines should be filled with antifreeze solution that contains a corrosion inhibitor. Some heat exchangers are made from more than one metal, in which case the seawater side may require an anode to protect it from galvanic corrosion.

Galvanic activity is also related to the relative size of the metals, so an aluminium rivet in a steel plate will corrode rapidly, but in the reverse case of a steel rivet in an aluminium plate the aluminium would corrode far more slowly due to its area. Painting the metal being protected is a useful method of preventing corrosion even when an anode is fitted, as is done on saildrive legs. Painting reduces the cathodic area, so improving anode life and efficiency of the protection.

An unusual example of galvanic corrosion has been seen on aluminium anchors. Lead is cast into the hollow anchor tip in order to provide the weight that causes it to set on the seabed. As can be seen in the galvanic series table a potential difference of about 0.5 volts exists between the two metals, with the result that the aluminium has corroded preferentially. The manufacturer has now coated the aluminium with a non-conducting material in an attempt to avoid this problem.

Where galvanic corrosion is particularly severe is in situations where an electric current passes through underwater components. A couple of examples are given here. In the first of these cases, the rudder and its fittings were severely corroded

Lead-filled aluminium anchor.

Rudder pintle 1. JAN LASSE EILERTSEN

Corrosion pit penetrating the aluminium.

Rudder pintle 2. JAN LASSE EILERTSEN

Wear of hydraulic hose.
JAN LASSE EILERTSEN

tery. This practice is now considered to offer no corrosion benefits and possible disadvantages, as in this case. It was subsequently found that both the engine and gearbox had suffered damage as a result of the incident.

The first photograph shows a skin fitting attached to a valve from which the outer flange has been corroded away and fallen off. Only the sealant prevented water from entering the boat.

In the next, another flange has been corroded through but in this instance it remained attached to the boat although the inner threaded section was released. The

due to the passage of electric current over a fairly brief period, although the exact time is not known. The result was spectacular loss of metal at the rudder pintles and of the stainless steel rudder itself. The triangular shape on the first pintle cannot be explained but may be an artefact of construction, with subsequent corrosion. The cause was found to be that the rubber sleeve on a hydraulic hose that formed part of the steering system had rubbed against a bare electric terminal until the reinforcing steel wire inside made contact. The hydraulic hose was connected directly to the rudder. A voltage of 12.7 volts was measured between the rudder and the engine block, which itself would have been connected to the driveshaft, completing the circuit when the boat was in the water.

In the second example a yacht's 12-volt supply inadvertently formed a circuit with several underwater fittings, when the owner mistakenly connected his anode to the positive side of the batteries. The damage shown occurred in about three weeks. A factor in the failure was that all seacocks were bonded (electrically connected) together and to the bat-

Seacock with handle. JON MARKOVITZ

Skin fitting with no flange. JON MARKOVITZ

Blakes seacock flange corrosion.
JON MARKOVITZ

The owner of the boat involved in this example of electrolytic corrosion is a renowned expert in marine electrical systems, and particularly batteries. During testing of the recovery rate of one of his batteries he ignored his own advice to always disconnect the negative terminal and instead disconnected the positive, leaving the live lead lying in the bilge. Unfortunately it contacted a skin fitting, with the result that a charge was applied to it. The photograph shows the condition of the fitting, originally in as-new condition, after 20 hours. The battery voltage had fallen to 10.5 volts during this period. MATT BONEY

outer flange of a Blakes seacock was corroded through.

Another example of a situation where electric cables may cause trouble is in marinas where several boats are connected to the mains supply. The earth wire in a three-wire cable connects adjacent boats electrically, even if the power to both is turned off. Assuming that the earth is connected to the sea via anodes, propeller and shaft or some other means, a circuit is made between the two boats. Any anodic metal will corrode preferentially, which can cause serious problems. In the worst situation one boat's anode, and within a short time its saildrive, could be protecting the boat next door. A galvanic isolator in the earth circuit will prevent this potential problem.

PITTING AND CREVICE CORROSION

Alloys that rely on the formation of a protective oxide film to prevent corrosion can suffer severe localized attack at points where the oxide film is breached. If a crevice, such as is formed in bolted joints, swaged fittings or nuts and bolts, is immersed in water, the oxygen content of the 'stagnant' water deep inside the crevice is lower than that of the fully aerated water on the outside. This difference causes the metal within the crevice to become active, corroding preferentially due to the fact that the active and passive metals have different galvanic potentials. The galvanic series in seawater table on page 96 show two potentials for stainless steel – the 'active' and 'passive' state. Pits are themselves small-scale crevices, as is the surface roughness in drawn rigging wire, accounting for the rust stains that can develop on them.

Passive films form where the oxygen content is higher but not where it is lower. The galvanic potentials of active and passive stainless steels are different, a galvanic cell is set up and the active metal corrodes.

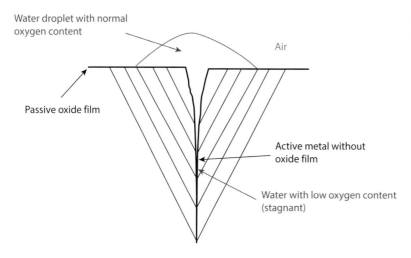

Crevice corrosion diagram.

Water droplet with normal oxygen content

Air

Passive oxide film

Active metal without oxide film

Water with low oxygen content (stagnant)

The most frequent complaint heard about stainless steels is that they are not 'stainless'. Nearly all of the rust staining seen around yacht fittings is caused by crevice corrosion. In this photograph crevices exist between the nut and bracket, nut and bolt, bracket and hull, tube and bracket. Even the roots of the threads in the bolt are crevices.

Permanently immersed, bolted fittings are particularly susceptible to crevice corrosion, as are many other pieces of equipment made in stainless steel where another component is immediately adjacent to them. Some examples are shown here.

The two approaches to avoiding crevice corrosion are to eliminate either or both of the crevice and the water. Wherever possible all bolted fittings should be bedded on a sealant that will both close the crevice and keep the water out. In some cases this is not possible, for example with swaged fittings on rigging wire, but filling them

Crevice corrosion in air.

Long, narrow flutes of crevice corrosion on a stainless steel shaft beneath the lands of a rubber cutless bearing.
MIKE WYLDE

Crevice corrosion damage on a stainless steel shaft on which the propeller has been mounted. The crevice was created where the propeller extended over the parallel part of the shaft, below, from the tapered part at top. Once the crevice was created around the circumference of the shaft it became self-perpetuating and continued inwards, parallel with the keyway. DAVID

A rope-stripper bolted to a propeller shaft. The bolting was uneven when made up, causing the two faces at the centre to be close together, creating a crevice, and also tilting the stripper relative to the shaft, creating another crevice. NICK HOPWOOD

Severe pitting due to crevice corrosion between a stainless steel propeller and its inner plastic bush. The boat was fitted with two propellers that were both affected similarly. GRAHAM ROBERTS

with Waxoyl or grease should exclude the water and prevent corrosion. Another way to prevent minor unsightly crevice corrosion staining, for example on rigging wire, is by polishing, which eliminates the fine crevices that cause it.

Bolts in wood are a particular problem as it is almost impossible to keep the wood dry. The bolted joint prevents oxygen from penetrating and corrosion results. The answer here is to use a different metal – silicon bronze being a far better choice.

SELECTIVE CORROSION

In this form of corrosion one element of an alloy is removed by corrosion, thus its alternative name is 'de-alloying'. In a form of galvanic corrosion on a micro scale, the more anodic metal is leached out, leaving the more noble metal behind. In the case of the dezincification of brass, perhaps the best-known form of de-alloying, the zinc is removed preferentially, leaving a spongy, weak copper-rich metal that has the typical pink colour of copper.

De-alloying also takes place in several other alloys, including cast iron, copper nickel and even duplex stainless steel.

In recent years dezincification of brass seacocks has become a matter of much discussion in the yachting press. In a few well-publicized cases boats have sunk or taken on water when dezincified skin fittings have failed.

De-alloying commences at the surface of the metal and progresses inwards, meaning that parts with thin sections can be affected severely whereas heavier sections may last for considerably longer. Skin fittings and hose tails with threaded ends are particularly at risk as the metal at the thread roots may be very thin, and several owners have experienced failures when leaning on hoses

when doing other work. The photo below, shows some small threaded ends cut from a skin fitting inside a ball valve.

In the photo at bottom a brass stern tube has suffered severe dezincification and metal loss, particularly problematic as in the event of failure it would be difficult to control inflow and the engine could not be used.

The photo opposite above is spectacular example of advanced dezincification in a hose tail taken from a Jeanneau. The whole

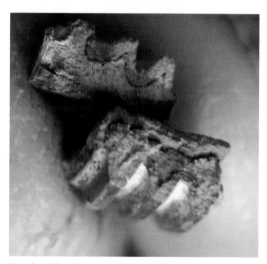

Dezincification on thread fragments.
DAVE CALVERT

Dezincification of stern tube.
GUIDO VILLAROSA

Dezincification of a hose tail.
CHRIS HOLDSTOCK

of the threaded region displays the red colour of the copper phase and its brittleness is evident.

The photo below shows a dezincified Flexofold propeller. This design of folding propeller relies on the meshing of gear teeth to keep the blades in registry. Dezincification of the teeth has caused the registry to be lost, leading to severe vibration in the drive train.

An example of serious dezincification in a seacock skin fitting is shown in the photo below. The flange has been ground off from outside the hull, evident at the top where the bright brass is revealed. At the lower part the copper colour of dezincification is very apparent, where it has penetrated from the bore right through the wall thickness. The strength of the fitting in this part was very low.

Many dezincified skin fittings have broken off when owners have leaned on them while carrying out maintenance on other parts of the installation. This is clearly a significant risk to the integrity of the vessel.

Dezincification of a folding propeller. PETE SCOWN

Severe dezincification of a seacock skin fitting. JOHN PRUDHOE

A different form of selective corrosion can occur in cast iron keels, when the iron is leached away, leaving graphite. This is known as graphitic corrosion or graphitization. Graphite is cathodic to iron and in grey iron, from which many keels are made, iron metal and graphite form a galvanic cell.

The reasons for its occurrence in seawater are unclear. The problem is recognized to occur in relatively mild environments such as soft waters with a slightly acidic pH, whereas seawater is slightly alkaline. Calm, non-flowing seawater, such as in some marinas, may be a contributory cause. Although not common, graphitic corrosion of yacht keels is encountered a few times each year.

In more aggressive environments, such as flowing seawater, corrosion may be more general, rather than graphitic in nature, but this is rare.

Below is an example of graphitic corrosion of a yacht keel. The surface layer

Graphitic corrosion of a keel. SLIPKNOT

of paint was rusty, which when removed revealed the appearance seen here. The graphite is soft and friable, easily rubbed away. The structure is that of the cast iron.

A rather more well-known example of selective corrosion is encountered by owners of welded stainless steel tanks, either in fuel tanks where water has been present for some time, or water tanks. When welds are made in general-purpose stainless steels that contain a small amount of carbon a problem known as 'sensitization' can take place. Some carbon in the heat-affected zone (HAZ) immediately adjacent to the weld combines with chromium in the alloy to form chromium carbides, which precipitate at the grain boundaries. The result is that the stainless steel in this area is deficient in chromium and thus corrodes preferentially when exposed to corrosive media. Additionally the grain boundaries become anodic to the grain itself, setting up a galvanic cell, leading to further corrosion. This condition is sometimes known as 'weld decay'.

The problem can be overcome by using grades of stainless steel with low carbon content (304L and 316L), or grades containing titanium, niobium or tantalum, which are preferential carbide formers. It is sometimes read that sensitization does not occur in welds of thin metals because chromium carbide precipitation cannot occur in the short time that the HAZ remains hot, but much experience in the yachting industry suggests otherwise.

STRESS CORROSION

The combination of static stress and corrosive chemicals can cause cracking in metals that are in a ductile condition. In many cases the chemical is not aggressive and is one that in other ways does not attack the alloy, for example seawater. Elevated temperatures, in excess of 50–60°C, are contributors to the problem, but it is well known at lower temperatures – for example it has been reported in metals used for implants in the human body.

In yachting it is seen in austenitic stainless steels and in 7000 series aluminium alloys.

Stress corrosion cracks are branched and propagate following a mostly intergranular path, generating an extremely rough, crystalline appearance. Close examination shows that unlike the single crack typical of fatigue, there are always several cracks radiating from a single point, sometimes likened to the shape of a tree.

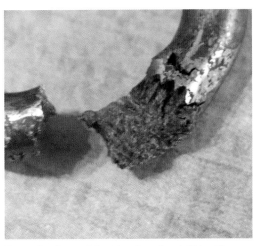

Branched cracking is clearly visible. It is assumed that the composition of this shackle was not what it should have been.

A small shackle in 316 stainless steel that was used in a highly stressed application securing reefing blocks at the foot of the mast. Three other shackles alongside this one remained in good condition without the corrosion that is evident here. Failure has taken place in the three most stressed locations.

This swivel attached 8mm chain to a 16kg anchor. It failed suddenly when subject to very low loads, suggesting that the metal was in a highly stressed condition.

A swaged fitting at the lower end of a shroud. Much of the surface of the fitting is rusty, which may indicate that its composition is inadequate for marine duty. At the upper end of the swage a rusty crack is visible. The metal here is highly stressed circumferentially due to the swaging procedure. Seawater and rainwater gather naturally in this area.

The crystalline appearance of the fracture faces indicates that the crack propagated on an intergranular path.

Light abrasion of the fitting to remove the surface corrosion reveals the typical branched cracking of stress-corrosion cracking.

HYDROGEN DAMAGE

Hydrogen molecules are extremely small by comparison with those of metals and in circumstances where hydrogen is being generated it is possible for the gas to diffuse into the metal, where it can lead to the generation of cracks under high stress. Fortunately the condition for this to occur is limited to high-strength steels, of which very few exist on boats. The one known exception is the re-galvanizing of Grade 70 chain. Before regalvanizing takes place the old zinc is stripped off in an acid bath, where hydrogen gas is generated. The resulting diffusion into the steel chain can result in a lowering of its strength. Most galvanizers will advise that more than one regalvanizing cycle should not be undertaken with this grade of chain. Grades 30 and 40 are not affected.

CHAPTER 11

Fatigue

Fatigue in metals suffers on account of its name, which many people associate with tiredness in humans. In fact, fatigue in metal components occurs when a crack grows through them until finally the force being transmitted exceeds the strength of the remaining material and it breaks. Fatigue in engineering terms has nothing to do with tiredness or obsolescence but is far more simply the growth of a crack through a highly stressed component. The consequence of this mechanism is that fatigue fractures always have a characteristic two-zone appearance – the part where the crack was propagating (growing) and the final fracture. In the vast majority of cases in engineering materials the final fracture will be ductile, but in a few materials, mainly some copper alloys, the final fracture can be brittle.

Fatigue fractures are often easy to identify because the fracture face has an appearance known as 'beach marks', rather like ripples in sand. The crack initiates at either one or a number of points and the crack radiates outwards, similar to the way in which ripples radiate outwards from a pebble dropped into water. This appearance is often seen in actual failures but in many, particularly where in long-term crack growth the two faces rub together, the detail of the beach marks is destroyed by polishing.

So why does fatigue occur? Failure is simply due to the repeated application of a load that would be insufficient to cause the metal to fail. We refer to this as cyclic stress, perhaps the most common example being the bending of a piece of wire backwards and forwards until it breaks. Extending this analogy a little further, if a small cut is made with a hacksaw in the centre of the section of wire being bent backwards and forwards it will break at the cut with fewer repetitions. This introduces the concept of a stress-raiser, the elimination of which is crucial to good design of any component that will see cyclic stress in service.

THE S/N CURVE

Diagrams that predict the fatigue characteristics of engineering metals are known as S/N curves, where S is stress and N is the number of cycles. As the stress level reduces the number of cycles required to cause fracture increases, on a logarithmic scale. Laboratory tests have been conducted for a wide variety of stress levels on all metals in common use and are freely available for reference. For steel, stainless steel and some other metals there is a threshold below which fatigue failure will never occur, known as the fatigue limit or endurance limit. Repetitive small stresses

The appearance of fatigue failure.

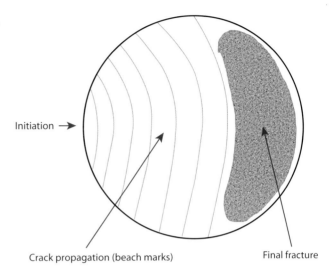

Initiation →

Crack propagation (beach marks)

Final fracture

A textbook fatigue fracture in one blade of a centrifugal compressor. In real-life fractures there is almost always polishing between faces as the crack propagates. In this example, as in laboratory-grown fractures, the two faces were held apart by the force of the gas flow that acted upwards in the photograph.

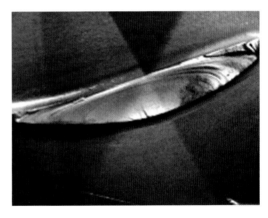

Fatigue SN curve showing fatigue limit

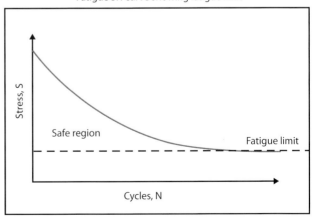

S/N curve for steel.

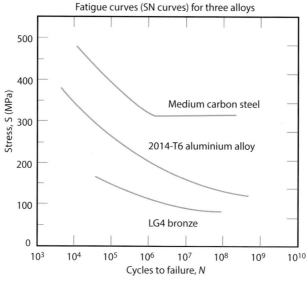

Fatigue curves (SN curves) for three alloys

S/N curve for three alloys.

below this value are in the 'safe region' and will not lead to fatigue failure. Designers of equipment made in steel aim to keep the stress in all components, whether keels, rudder stocks, rigging or engine components, within the safe region.

In many other metals, notably copper and aluminium alloys, there is no fatigue limit and small stress repetitions will eventually lead to failure. Alloys with no fatigue limit need to be selected with care, using a variety of compositions and tempers that match fatigue performance to the duty to ensure long-term reliability.

CHARACTERISTICS OF FATIGUE

A description of fatigue failure often expressed is that they were 'sudden', 'out of the blue', or 'with no warning'. The reality is that the crack may have been growing for months or even years, failure taking place when the stress in the remaining part of the metal exceeded its strength.

The main difference between the 'typical appearance' diagram shown and real fractures in engineering components is that the final fracture area is usually quite small. Well-engineered components everywhere are designed with safety factors that allow the items to be capable of carrying far greater forces than they see in service. The result is that the crack will grow through anything up to 90 per cent of the cross-sectional area before the item finally fails due to overload.

The fractured nut and bolt shown next was one of five used to connect one of the floats of a trimaran to the main hull. A fatigue crack has grown downwards from the 11 o'clock position in the photograph until the final fracture occurred at the crescent-shaped feature, lower right. There is some evidence of a shear lip here, typical of ductile fractures. Beach marks are only vaguely evident, typical of fatigue fractures in the real world. The position of the crack at the first thread of the nut is absolutely characteristic, being the position of highest stress in bolted joints. Although both nut and bolt are made from

Fatigued bolt. JOHN BLAIKLOCK

316 stainless steel there is evident corrosion due to restricted oxygen levels within the crack and the joint.

Next shown is a failed connecting rod from a Volvo Penta engine. The problem here was that the nut on the other connecting rod bolt became loose, transferring the majority of the stress to the one that remained tight. This caused the big-end cap to undergo cyclic bending as the engine ran, initiating a fatigue crack at the point near the head of the remaining bolt. The initiation of the crack has multiple origins, visible as small steps adjacent to the bolt head. These are known as 'ratchet marks'. The crack propagated

Fatigued connecting rod.

along a face towards the camera, creating visible beach marks despite some polishing between the adjacent faces.

Finally the stress was too much for the remaining metal to sustain and the connecting rod broke at the bright area at the extreme left, also creating a shear lip where the metal has been pulled outwards.

STRESS CONCENTRATION

Achieving a design in which stresses are always within the safe region would be simple if everything was regular in shape. Unfortunately this is rarely the case and most engineering components include section changes, keyways, bolt holes, threads and a myriad other factors that increase the stress locally, to levels that may be within the 'danger area'. The diagram overleaf shows the effect of a change of section on a shaft. Where there is no radius the local stress may be very high and sufficient to initiate a fatigue crack, whereas where a fillet radius is included the stress will be raised but not to dangerous levels.

Examples of stress concentration in yacht rigging are quite common at the terminations, where the cable is attached by swaging, an operation that presses the soft metal of the fitting into the lay of the wire at high pressure. If the wire is subsequently bent at the end of the fitting the local stress concentration is increased and there is a high likelihood that fatigue will initiate there if exposed to cyclic stress.

One common cause is that due to a problem with the swaging machine dies the fitting is not straight, known as 'banana' swages. Here the loading of the wire is concentrated at one side of the fitting, increasing the stress locally to a higher figure than the rig designer intended. It can be seen that once the rig is tight there

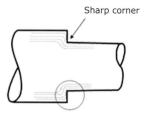

Sharp corner

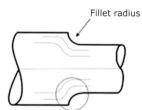

Fillet radius

Stress concentration.

Abrupt change
Stress 'flow lines' compressed
High stress concentration

Smoother change
'Flow lines' less compressed
Reduced stress concentration

will be a tendency for the wire to be pulled more in line with the ruler, causing the upper side of the wire to see increased tension levels. Banana swages are often made using a machine that is too small for the job, requiring too many passes that cause both bending of the swage due to excessive friction on one side and excessive work hardening, which can cause embrittlement.

In some cases a fitting may be displaced, is in the case of a spreader end where the wire has been displaced to a severe extent, again increasing the tensile stress at one side.

Next we see the forestay and swaged fitting of a yacht that was berthed on an exposed mooring subject to some swell, with an excessively slack rig. Fatigue cracks grew through the individual wires of the forestay

Deformed shroud at spreader.

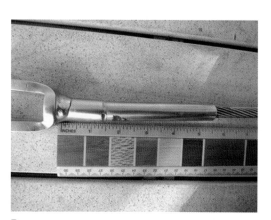

Banana swage. GRYPHON

over a period of time until ultimately the few remaining strands were too few to hold up the rig and it collapsed. Beach marks are clearly visible on many strands in the wire, particularly at the top. These strands are tarnished and have evidently been fractured for some time. Those at the bottom are bright and probably failed in overload. Note that the failure took place near the end of the swaged fitting, where the bending stress is at its highest.

I was sent a failed shroud to examine. It was known that the rig had been very

Fatigued forestay.

Beach marks on wire ends.

slack for some time, with the result that a couple of shroud wires had fractured and were protruding from the swaged fitting. I examined the wire ends with a microscope and could identify beach marks on one and polishing on the other, both indicating fatigue. Finally I slit the swaged fitting open to reveal that several more wires were fractured inside. This owner was fortunate that his mast and rig remained in place, as no doubt the other wires were also fatigued but not yet fractured. Again, the wire fractures took place at the point in the whole assembly where the stress was concentrated by the bending action at the limit of the swage.

Swage cut open.

A couple of years ago we were berthed adjacent to a very well-found Italian boat fitted out for long-distance cruising. We met the owner and enjoyed an evening with him and his crew. A few days later we had moved on and met him again, in very different circumstances. On passage between islands a shroud had failed, his mast had gone over the side and his cruise had been ruined.

Loss of the rig was initiated by the fracture of a tang connecting a lower spreader to the mast. This had been fabricated from sheet stainless steel about 6mm in thickness. The design of this component did not allow articulation and its repeated bending was probably responsible for the failure.

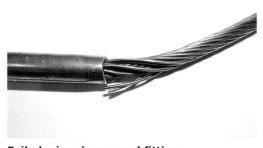

Failed wires in swaged fitting.

Dismasted yacht.

The fitting had been riveted directly to the mast without toggles, allowing bending stresses to act directly upon it. The fracture face is characteristic of fatigue. The crack initiated simultaneously at a number of points along the lower edge, as evidenced by the seven or eight vertical marks, known as 'ratchets'. The crack had been growing for some time, forming beach marks as it propagated and finally failing along the top edge. While the crack was growing, mild corrosion was able to progress and cause the typical orange-brown colour. The bright line at the top of the face represents the area remaining when final fracture took place.

Jefa Steering Cable

A steering cable on a Hanse 400 yacht failed off the west coast of Portugal. The cable assembly was from a twin wheel steering system, comprising lengths of chain at each wheel and a shorter length at the mid-point for the autopilot. The chains were connected together by four 7 × 7 cables each 5mm in diameter.

The cable was broken or damaged at four points, each corresponding with the position of a sheave, which were of 10.0cm diameter. The cable had failed at each sheave – one had parted completely and

Mast tang with beach marks.

Steering cable arrangement.

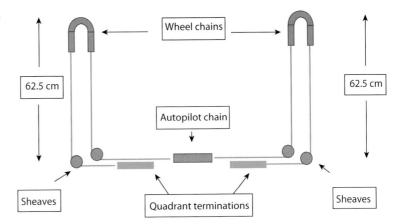

the other three had suffered fractures of several strands. In one case only four or five strands remained intact. Examination showed the fractured ends to be polished but beach marks were not evident. The cables were otherwise in good condition, without wear.

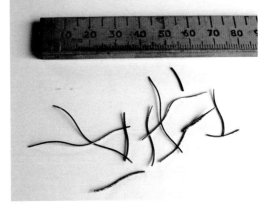

Cable fragments.

Fractured cable.

Fatigued strands in cable.

In each of the four damaged or fractured areas there were many breaks in the wires. In some cases individual wires had fractured several times, creating short pieces of 20–40mm length that were partially embedded in the lay of the cable. Similar short lengths of wire had been found in the bilge of the boat.

The cable failed by fatigue due to repeated flexing and straightening at the sheaves during operation. The cause was that 7 × 7 cable had been installed instead of the correct 7 × 19 construction. Minimum sheave diameters are specified for each cable construction and it can be seen

Table showing minimum ratios of sheave diameter D and cable diameter d

	Desirable minimum diameter		Critical minimum diameter	
	7 × 7 cable	7 × 19 cable	7 × 7 cable	7 × 19 cable
D:d	42:1	24:1	28:1	18:1
For 5mm cable	21.6cm	11.9cm	14.0cm	8.9cm

Cable construction.

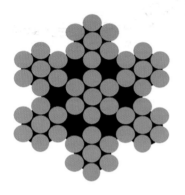 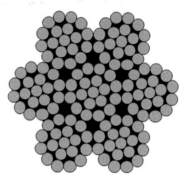

7 × 7 cable construction   7 × 19 cable construction

that 7 × 7 cable is inappropriate for 10cm sheaves.

Halyard Wrap

Another form of fatigue fracture in wire cables is the one involved in 'halyard wraps'. With roller-furling genoas the jib halyard must form a significant angle with

Halyard wrap.

the forestay to prevent it from wrapping around the forestay during furling. If this happens the wire becomes alternately wound and unwound, leading to a form of fatigue known as high-stress, low-cycle. Wire forestays can fail by this mechanism in only about ten cycles. It can be seen that the inner core wire of this 1 × 19 cable has been twisted excessively whereas the outer has been unwound. Although the halyard itself usually continues to provide some support it is not unknown for the mast to go overboard due to this failure.

FATIGUE PREVENTION

The common description of fatigue failures is that they 'suddenly broke'. This is actually not true, as a crack always forms before final fracture takes place. Although stainless steels are no more prone to fatigue than is any other steel in its soft condition, the problem is that in yachts we apply high cyclic loads to relatively soft stainless steels, often in badly designed circumstances. It may be difficult for the average yachtsman to determine whether the design is good or not, so a combination of critical assessment and inspection is required, which is exactly the same as for professionals. All chain plates, toggles, swaged fittings, T-balls and their sockets, rigging screws and any other highly loaded parts should be examined, first for any sign that the load is being applied so that one side is more heavily stressed than another, and second for the presence of cracks. Annual inspection is usually considered to be sufficient.

So far as prevention is concerned, the yacht owner should ensure that the rig of his boat is kept tight, make regular checks of components known to be at risk, such as all wires, engine mountings, coupling bolts, forestay attachments and suchlike. In particular, it is essential that all standing rigging is fitted with toggles that prevent the direct application of stresses to the mast or fittings.

Visual inspection is usually sufficient to identify problems such as broken rigging wires and misaligned components. Non-destructive inspection techniques such as dye penetrant methods are available and can be used without specialist knowledge, but the small size of most components mitigates against their usefulness. Inspection methods are discussed in Chapter 13.

CHAPTER 12

Combinations of Failure Modes

In many cases in the real world there is more than one factor at work when components fail. One has already been covered in the corrosion section, namely stress-corrosion fractures. Failures by this mechanism would not occur as a result of either one of stress or corrosion but in combination they proved fatal.

Corrosion fatigue is another example. The fatigue resistance of most metals when tested in vacuum is considerably higher than when tested in air, and things get worse when they are subjected to corrosive conditions. The action of corrosive media at the fatigue crack tip exacerbates the situation, with the result that the fatigue limit ceases to exist and metals even within the 'safe zone' are liable to failure.

A situation that can be very problematic in moorings, where the metals used are carbon steels, perhaps with an initial galvanized coating, is the combination of wear and corrosion, known as corrosive wear. The cause of the exceptional wear rates that can result from this combination is as follows. Initially any galvanizing, lubricant or paint films are worn away by wave action. As soon as the steel beneath the coating is exposed it begins to corrode in the seawater, forming rust. Rust is relatively soft and friable and is easily worn away by contact with the adjacent part of

the chain or shackle. This constant cycle of corrosion followed by wear can result in the failure of moorings in less than one season, particularly where the metal used has poor corrosion resistance.

Take, for example, the history of *Daisy*, a 19ft boat on a half-tide mooring on the Menai Strait. Daisy's mooring comprises lengths of 12mm galvanized mild steel chain connected together beneath the water and/or mud with a 12mm galvanized mild steel shackle, which had the largest pin that would pass through the links of the chain. The mooring was rated at 2 tonnes. After four years of ownership it was noticed that some wear had taken place in the upper half metre of chain and it was replaced, using a new shackle. Within six months the shackle had wasted severely and the mooring failed, casting *Daisy* loose. The shackle was recovered and photographed.

The shackle has suffered general corrosion that has led to loss of metal throughout, but the serious wear adjacent to the chain in the bow of the shackle and between the pin and its eyes is due to the combination of corrosion and wear. It was suggested that there was some galvanic component due to the attached Monel seizing wire but I believe this to be relatively too small to drive a corrosion reaction to any extent.

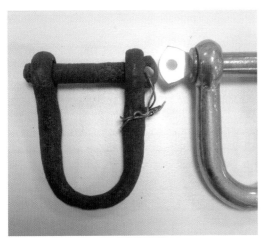

Corrosive wear of shackle. CHRIS JONES

Corrosive wear of chain.

The second example was found on a mooring for a small boat in Pollensa, Mallorca. In the Mediterranean there is no significant tide but the 8mm mooring chain has been dragged from one side of the mooring sinker to the other due to wind action. The dragging action has caused wear of the chain against the sand of the seabed, with the spectacular result shown above.

Corrosive wear of pin. CHRIS JONES

CHAPTER 13

Inspection

Although the metallurgy of boating equipment is complex and varied, it is the case that every problem or failure described in this book is visible to the naked eye, or at worst with a small magnifying glass of around ×8 magnification. Unfortunately it is evident that many of the failures described were not immediately obvious before they occurred, requiring specific inspection techniques to discover them. However, none of these is beyond the capability of the owner or skipper, provided he knows what he is looking for. The great majority of failures occur due to either corrosion caused by the saline composition of seawater, or fatigue caused by the cyclic motion imparted by either or both of the wind and the waves. It might be imagined that metal parts that are permanently immersed are more likely to suffer corrosion, but in fact this is not always the case. Similarly, fatigue affects both underwater parts such as rudder stocks as well as masts and fittings.

I have therefore described the principal methods by which premature failures may be detected before the event by equipment type.

ANCHORS

Anchors are solidly constructed, the best examples lasting almost indefinitely and it might be imagined that inspection is un-necessary. Several types of deterioration are known, the worst being fracture of the shanks of cheaply made copies of well-known models such as the one shown on page 26. In this case the crack grew progressively and would have been revealed by careful inspection, quite possibly for months or even years before it failed.

The hinges of articulated anchors wear over years of use, resulting in poor setting due to the presentation of the tip to the seabed at an excessive angle. This type of anchor should be retired when wear has progressed to excessive levels.

ANODES

An anode that is doing its job correctly will corrode while protecting the components to which it is connected. If an anode is not corroding away the cause should be investigated, as the corrosion rate of zinc or aluminium not connected to another metal in seawater is relatively low. With a large cathode the rate of anode loss can be high, even to the extent that none remains partway through a yachting season; in this case painting the cathode to reduce its active area, or doubling up the anode size, may be necessary. It is widely advised that anodes be replaced before a new season when they are half-consumed, to ensure a full season's service.

CHAIN

The two main degradation modes of chain are general and galvanic corrosion and wear. General corrosion results in white deposits of zinc hydroxide due to permanent immersion of the chain in water, typically in the anchor locker (page 74). Galvanic corrosion occurs in protecting the steel of the chain's construction and/or stainless steel swivels and shackles connecting it to the anchor. Zinc loss adjacent to stainless steel fittings is slow: in five years the final three links of my anchor chain have gradually turned black, then red, as the zinc was lost. Conversely, the thickness of zinc provided in modern chain manufacture can be very low and new chain that I bought some years ago was rusted throughout after three seasons. The best option here is to have it regalvanized at a cost of about 30 per cent of new chain.

Wear takes place primarily between links, and in some cases can take place quite rapidly. The rule of thumb here is that a loss in thickness of up to 10 per cent is acceptable, but beyond that the chain should be scrapped.

C-LINKS

Most C-links are made from either mild or alloy steel, although there are some stainless steel versions. The steel ones are provided with a zinc coating, probably electroplated rather than hot dip galvanizing, which is consumed at a high rate. Regular inspection is required as the unprotected link can corrode rapidly (page 75).

KEELS

Corrosion is the primary enemy of iron keels, for which regular painting is the favoured protection method. Grit blasting followed by immediate application of epoxy primer and top coat is the most effective means of protection, but lesser methods such as angle grinding followed by conventional painting are widely used. Inspection is limited to selecting areas for touching up until more major coating can be undertaken.

Keels that are attached to the hull by bolts may need more rigorous inspection. If rusty water is found in the bilges the source is likely to be water penetrating via the keel bolts: this indicates that their sealing has broken down and may also result in galvanic corrosion between the bolts and the iron of the keel. In these circumstances rebedding the hull onto the keel using new sealant is advisable.

Rust may be seen at the external joint between the bolted keel and hull. In most cases this is not a cause for concern and can be addressed by the application of sealant. Ideally this should be done with the boat hanging in the hoist slings to open up any clearance between the two. Applying sealant with the weight of the boat resting on the keel is unlikely to be successful.

MASTS

Elderly masts are frequently found to have suffered galvanic corrosion between the aluminium of the extrusion and rivets, fittings and, in particular, the casting that forms the base of the mast. In some cases it is the fittings that corrode, in others it is the mast itself. Aluminium alloys form white deposits when they corrode, so any unexpected white stains revealed by inspection should be investigated further. The cause is often that water is able to lodge in gaps and crevices, in which case sealants may be useful to close them.

By far the greatest cause of fatigue in rigging components is under-tightening of the rig. Cyclic movement occurs continuously, not only when the boat is sailing but also when it is berthed. This soon results in the millions of cycles needed for low-stress, high-cycle fatigue fracture. Rig tension should be checked regularly, either using a gauge or an extension method as advised by mast manufacturers.

Mast extrusions rarely suffer fatigue problems but the fittings used to hold them up are very susceptible. T-ball shroud ends lock into plates that are typically riveted to the mast. These plates often suffer fatigue cracks and on occasion these continue to propagate into the mast itself as movement of the plate increases. Stemball fittings are used in a similar way to connect the forestay to the masthead fitting and both these and T-balls need to be inspected carefully for fatigue cracks, particularly at any changes of section. Ideally this should be carried out annually.

In some cases shrouds are attached to masts using tangs that are riveted to the mast section. There should always be a tang between the shroud's swaged fitting and the toggle to allow full 360-degree articulation of any movement. A considerable risk of fatigue failure exists where no toggle is fitted (page 112).

PROPELLERS

The majority of yacht propellers are made in an alloy known as Manganese Bronze, which despite its name is actually a brass with minor additions of other metals (page 57). This composition makes it susceptible to dezincification. Inspection for this degradation process is firstly by colour, looking for the pinkness that indicates loss of the zinc phase. An area of one or more propeller blades is abraded back to clean bare metal using papers of around 180 grit. Where any pinkness is seen it is worthwhile continuing the abrasion process, as it is quite common for it to extend only a short depth into the metal. In severe cases the metal will appear dark red throughout, in which case it is often seen that chips of metal have been lost at the blade edges and tips. When struck lightly with a small hammer a sound propeller will ring, whereas one badly affected by dezincification will emit a dull thud.

PROPELLER SHAFTS

Austenitic stainless steel shafts usually have excellent corrosion resistance but when the boat has been stationary for extended periods it is possible for crevice corrosion to occur between it and any other component that is in close contact with it. Common locations for this problem are beneath the flutes of a rubber cutless bearing, the propeller and rope cutters (pages 98–99). Rotation of the shaft will reveal the first of these but more extensive disassembly is needed for the others. It has been seen that a similar problem will take place beneath marine organisms and even splashes of antifouling paint that have fallen onto the shaft, which should be removed to inspect beneath.

RUDDER STOCKS

From time to time the yachting press publicises the loss of rudders, usually on specific makes of boats and most probably with spade rudders. In this design, which has no lower bearing, all of the rudder loads are applied in bending to the stock where it emerges from the hull. Unfortunately some manufacturers have introduced a change in section at this point, the stock diameter reducing where it enters the rudder. This is an ideal circumstance for the initiation and propagation of a fatigue crack, which in the cases I have seen reported was undoubtedly the cause of loss of the rudder. This area needs to be inspected most carefully, ideally using a non-destructive inspection technique such as dye-penetrant. In one or two known examples a GRP layer covers the change in section, necessitating it to be cut away.

SEACOCKS

Many seacocks have been made in 60/40 brass that makes them susceptible to dezincification on immersion in seawater. Inspection is made in a similar way to that described for propellers, abrading the metal to detect pinkness. However, severe dezincification offers the greatest threat to strength at points of thinnest section, such as threaded regions of the skin fitting or hose tail, where inspection by colour is problematic. These areas can be checked by tapping with a hammer using a screwdriver or similar tool as a drift to direct the blow to the area of interest. Several owners have experienced complete failure of seacock assembles when they inadvertently leaned on them or their attached hoses when doing other work (page 101). This suggests that applying vigorous loads to all such assemblies before launching at the beginning of the season is well worth doing.

SHACKLES

Most shackles undergo fluctuating loads when being used for sailing but these are relaxed when the boat is berthed. Thus fatigue failures are relatively rare. Some are under constant load at all times, leading to the possibility that stress corrosion failure may take place. The usual conditions quoted for stress corrosion are a temperature in excess of 60°C, which may seem unlikely in a northern European climate. In fact, when the sun is shining on metal components they may achieve surprisingly high temperatures. Failure of highly loaded shackles could have serious consequences and it is well worth inspecting them occasionally, looking out for branched cracking (page 103).

STERN GLANDS

Traditional stern glands with soft packing are made from bronze, so need little attention to ensure their long life. Increasingly, new designs that either include stainless steel parts in contact with seawater or rubber parts that lie against the propeller shaft may suffer from crevice corrosion. Since these components are responsible for keeping water out of the boat in this critical area it is well worth inspecting thoroughly before launching. Crevice corrosion pitting may appear minor but over a period of days or weeks unattended may allow sufficient ingress of water to sink the boat.

SWAGED FITTINGS

Fittings applied to the ends of wire rope for standing rigging are applied using a process known as swaging, in which the tubular fitting is compressed heavily, extruding metal into the lay of the rope that is inside it. The metal of the swage is highly stressed and, particularly at the lower end of shrouds, salty water readily flows into the top of the fitting. Constant evaporation of the water concentrates the saline solution, creating ideal conditions for stress-corrosion cracking (page 104). All swaged fittings should be inspected for cracking regularly, at the top end up the mast annually and on deck whenever convenient.

The point where the wire emerges from the swaged fitting is a stress raiser. If the wire vibrates excessively due to slackness there is a likelihood that fatigue cracks will initiate at this point (page 111). Wires will fracture one by one, causing the broken ends to protrude from the lay of the rope. Inspection of on-deck fittings by eye and those up the mast by binoculars should look for any strands protruding, in which case which action to replace the shroud should be taken immediately.

WIRE ROPE AND CABLE

Wire rope is made in a variety of different lays for different purposes (page 46). Ropes that are required to bend around sheaves of small diameter such as steering cables and running rigging comprise many small diameter wire strands, for example 7 × 19, whereas ropes that remain largely straight but need maximum strength, typical of standing rigging, are 1 × 19. Inspection should determine firstly that the rope in service is appropriate for the duty. Ropes that have long service lives will begin to develop fatigue cracks even when they have been correctly specified for the duty. With halyards it may be noticed that some strands are protruding from the rope, possibly injuring the hands.

Steering systems are largely out of sight, requiring some effort to inspect, but it is advisable to carry this out from time to time, concentrating on the areas around turning sheaves.

DYE PENETRANT INSPECTION

Examination of components susceptible to fatigue by eye, or with a magnifying glass of around ×8 may succeed in finding cracks but this would be a very tedious way to inspect a complete boat. The most effective method of finding fatigue cracks is when they have only just started and are very small. The method selected needs to: be affordable, leave the components being examined unaffected and in place, and be easy to interpret by the non-specialist. One of the most versatile methods is dye penetrant testing. Very simply, a strongly coloured dye is sprayed onto the component and allowed to penetrate any cracks. A white titanium dioxide powder in suspension, known as 'developer', is then sprayed on and the dye that has remained in the crack is drawn out, staining the white layer and revealing its location.

Dye penetrant inspection is rarely required on a regular basis on a yacht but in some cases a particular class may have a reputation for failures of a component and in these cases it can be justified to inspect. The diagram shows typical high-stress areas in shafts and chain plates where occasional dye penetrant examination can be worthwhile.

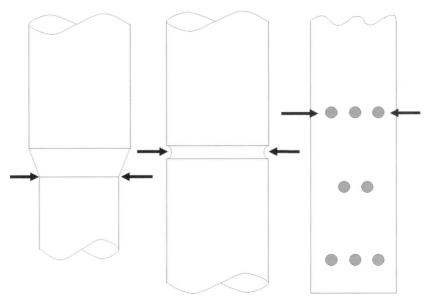

High-stress areas in shafts and chain plates.

Fatigue cracks in a propeller hub as revealed by dye penetrant crack detection. The faint purple lines towards the centre of the photograph were invisible by eye.

Index

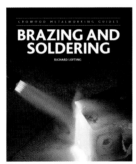

Brazing and Soldering
RICHARD LOFTING
ISBN 978 1 84797 836 3
128pp, 300 illustrations

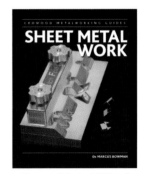

Sheet Metal Work
DR MARCUS BOWMAN
ISBN 978 1 84797 778 6
160pp, 450 illustrations

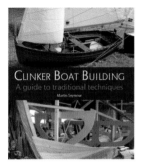

Clinker Boat Building
MARTIN SEYMOUR
ISBN 978 1 84797 334 4
160pp, 180 illustrations

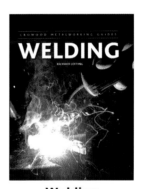

Welding
RICHARD LOFTING
ISBN 978 1 84797 432 7
160pp, 280 illustrations

Engineering Materials
HENRY TINDELL
ISBN 978 1 84797 679 6
160pp, 230 illustrations

In case of difficulty ordering, please contact the Sales Office:

The Crowood Press
Ramsbury
Wiltshire
SN8 2HR
UK
Tel: 44(0) 1672 520320

enquiries@crowood.com

www.crowood.com